Early praise for *Programming Crystal*

One of the best introductions to programming with Crystal that I've read. Clear examples and excellent explanations make this a must-read for anyone looking to get started with Crystal.

➤ **Dary Merckens**
   CTO, Gunner Technology

This book has something for everyone. Real stories can motivate adoption and remind us how proud we all must be about this language. It's a nice introduction for the language itself and to the existing ecosystem that programmers with even little experience will enjoy. Even people that have been using Crystal for a while will find new information in the book. I did!

➤ **Brian J. Cardiff**
   Research and Dev Lead, Manas.Tech

Ruby's performance level and concurrency support have troubled me for some time. Here, the authors have definitely encouraged me to convert to Crystal: I got a sort of click experience when I read about Crystal's nil-safety and my eyes went a little wide as I realized what an enormous improvement this was.

➤ **Nigel Lowry**
   Company Director, Lemmata Ltd.

Programming Crystal

Create High-Performance, Safe, Concurrent Apps

Ivo Balbaert
Simon St. Laurent

The Pragmatic Bookshelf

Raleigh, North Carolina

Our Pragmatic books, screencasts, and audio books can help you and your team create better software and have more fun. Visit us at *https://pragprog.com.*

The team that produced this book includes:

Publisher: Andy Hunt
VP of Operations: Janet Furlow
Managing Editor: Susan Conant
Development Editor: Andrea Stewart
Copy Editor: Nancy Rapoport
Indexing: Potomac Indexing, LLC
Layout: Gilson Graphics

For sales, volume licensing, and support, please contact *support@pragprog.com.*

For international rights, please contact *rights@pragprog.com.*

ISBN-13: 978-1-68050-286-2
Book version: P1.0—February 2019

Contents

Part II — Building Blocks

Part IV — Appendices

Preface

Crystal[1] combines the elegant coding of dynamic languages like Ruby or Python with the safety and blazing performance of a natively compiled language like Go or Rust. Ruby[2]—a very similar language—is sometimes said to be a programmer's best friend. Crystal is a language for both humans and computers.

Who This Book Is For

This book is for you if you're a developer who'd like to learn more about what Crystal has to offer and why it will be a useful tool in your software toolbelt.

If you already know Ruby, switching to Crystal will be almost effortless—you should feel at home quickly. You can reuse a lot of knowledge, established principles, and practices from the Ruby world in your Crystal projects. You just need to pay some attention to the types of certain variables, and the compiler will help you out with that.

You don't, however, need Ruby experience to get the most from this book. Crystal is also approachable to newcomers from other programming languages, or for newcomers to programming. This book assumes you're familiar with basic programming terms and concepts. You'll have a head start if you come from another object-oriented language or a statically compiled language.

What's in This Book

This book teaches the basics of Crystal with an emphasis on how its developers structured its design to make it perform so well.

As Crystal is a recent addition to the programming world, convincing companies and individuals to use it is trickier than promoting familiar tools. To help

---

1.　https://crystal-lang.org/
2.　https://www.ruby-lang.org/en/

deal with those challenges, you'll find discussions about real-world use cases, entitled "A Company's Story Crystallized," at the end of each chapter.

The book is organized into three parts:

Part I — Getting Started

We'll begin by going over all the good reasons you should use Crystal. Then you'll set up a working Crystal environment and work through a mini-tutorial.

Chapter 1: Diving into Crystal

First, you'll learn the main reasons for Crystal's success: it combines human-readable syntax with native code execution performance. You'll get a first impression of Crystal code, and you'll see why Crystal focuses on types, potentially saving you from lots of runtime errors.

Chapter 2: Crystal Foundations

This chapter teaches the core of the Crystal programming language through examples you can try in the Crystal playground. You'll get an overview of variables and types, and how to structure data. You'll explore logical structures and build simple methods, classes, and modules.

Part II — Building Blocks

This part examines the building blocks of Crystal in much greater depth: variable types, basic and compound data types, control structures, methods, classes, modules, generating docs, testing frameworks, and code formatting.

Chapter 3: Typing Variables and Controlling the Flow

Simple and compound types are the heart of Crystal. Control flow will probably be familiar, but using union types offers some new possibilities here, for example in exception handling.

Chapter 4: Organizing Code in Methods and Procs

Crystal adds type-based method overloading and the multiple dispatch technique, which is one of the keys to Crystal's speed. We'll also explore how procs, pointers to blocks of code, can be used in very flexible ways, and how Crystal adds some nice syntax sugar.

Chapter 5: Using Classes and Structs

Crystal's type hierarchy is laid out here, together with information about when to prefer structs over classes. You'll see in the type hierarchy how carefully the types were designed to deliver performance. Also, we'll go over visibility of methods, inheritance, and abstract types.

Chapter 6: Working with Modules

Modules structure code by defining namespaces, but also, as in Ruby and Dart, enable you to mix in code and methods of other types. We'll discuss the appropriate use of require, include, and extend.

Chapter 7: Managing Projects

Here you'll analyze a typical generated project structure, and we'll examine how to write tests using the built-in spec framework. You'll learn how to include external libraries, how to generate documentation, and how to benchmark your code.

Part III — Advanced Features

Once you've learned the heart of the language, you can explore Crystal's features for maximizing code reuse, as well as sharing code and data.

Chapter 8: Advanced Features

Here you'll dive into macros—Crystal's mechanism to generate code at compile-time. Then we'll discuss binding to C libraries and how Crystal implements concurrency through lightweight fibers communicating data over channels. A unified API called crystal-db gives you an easy way to access databases and SQL, as well as NoSQL.

Chapter 9: Web Frameworks and the Shard Ecosystem

Here you'll explore Kemal and other web frameworks that aim to provide Rails-like functionality. We'll also discuss some important packages, shards in Crystal parlance, in various application areas.

In the appendices, you'll find installation instructions, tips for porting Ruby code to Crystal, and answers to the exercises and questions presented throughout the book.

How to Read This Book

It's best to read the book from start to finish. But if you know that you want to learn Crystal and you want to get moving quickly:

- Set up Crystal and choose an editor, or use the Playground: see *Installing Crystal on Your Machine*, on page 194 and *Working with Crystal Playground*, on page 200.

- Work through the tutorial in Chapter 2.

- Part II should give you most of what you need to code in Crystal.

- You can skim Part III, looking for features that seem especially relevant to your needs, or come back to Chapter 1 to read some Crystal motivations.

- Or read an inspiring company story at the end of each chapter.

Throughout the book, you can follow along by executing and otherwise experimenting with the snippets in the code files accompanying each chapter (see code/chapter_name). You'll find all the code shown in the book in the accompanying code files.

Practice is the best way to learn a new language, so in every chapter you'll find "Your Turn" exercises where you can try out your new skills and explore different ways of solving problems. When you're finished with each exercise, you'll find example solutions in the appendix and the code download.

Conventions Used in This Book

The following notation conventions are used throughout the book.

A # => precedes the output or results of executing a code snippet.

```
p 2 + 2    # => 4
```

In order to keep code short, we'll sometimes omit the p, puts or print in the book like this:

```
2 + 2    # => 4
```

The Crystal Playground environment (see *Working with Crystal Playground*, on page 200) shows the values and types of all expressions, so you don't need to tell the program explicitly to print. Use p, puts, or print, however, to produce output in another editor or IDE.

Some code files contain lines that compile into an error. This is on purpose because errors can be very educational. Examining these error messages carefully gives you a good indication of what went wrong, and some messages even point to remedies. Comment out these lines if you want the file as a whole to compile and run.

Almost all of the errors happen while you're compiling code, and we'll indicate them with

```
Error: message
```

after the offending line. A runtime error, an error that happens while the program is running, which is rare in Crystal, will appear as follows:

```
Runtime error: message
```

If something needs to be invoked on the command-line terminal, you'll see a $ sign preceding it in the text:

```
$ crystal build hello_world.cr
```

Some Ruby conventions are also used in Crystal:

- A # sign indicates a comment.
- In an expression such as Shape#perim, a # indicates the perim method on an instance of Shape.

Web Resources and Feedback

Programming Crystal's official home on the web is the Programming Crystal home page[3] at the Pragmatic Bookshelf website. From there you can order electronic or paper copies of the book and download sample code. You can also offer feedback by submitting errata entries[4] for the book.

Downloading Sample Code

The sample code for the book is available from Pragmatic[5] and at GitHub.[6]

Throughout the book, listings begin with their filename, set apart from the actual code by a gray or light teal background. For example, the following listing comes from code/crystal_new/variables.cr:

```
crystal_new/variables.cr
str = "What a beautiful mineral!"
str1 = "What a
        beautiful mineral!" # multi-line string
```

If you are reading the ebook, clicking the little gray box above the code extracts directly downloads that snippet. With the sample code in hand, you are ready to get started.

---

3. https://pragprog.com/book/crystal/crystal
4. https://pragprog.com/titles/crystal/errata
5. https://pragprog.com/titles/crystal/source_code
6. https://github.com/Ivo-Balbaert/programming_crystal

Acknowledgments

Many people have contributed to what's good in this book. The problems and errors that remain are the authors' alone.

Thanks to everyone at the Pragmatic Bookshelf. Thanks to Dave Thomas and Andy Hunt for creating a fun platform for writing technical books and for betting on the passions of their authors.

Thanks to our editors, Jackie Carter, Katie Dvorak, Susannah Davidson Pfalzer, and especially Andrea Stewart. Their advice made the book way better.

Thanks to our technical reviewers for all your comments and helpful suggestions, including Antonio Cangiano, Brian J. Cardiff, Pieter-Jan Coenen, Ashish Dixit, Kevin Gisi, Derek Graham, Gábor László Hajba, Michael Keeling, Nigel Lowry, Dary Merckens, Sean Miller, Russ Olsen, Frank Ruiz, Peter Schols, Gianluigi Spagnuolo, and Tom Verbesselt. Your remarks made this book so much better.

Thanks to all the people who posted suggestions in the forum and on the book's errata page.

Thanks to Ary Borenszweig and the Crystal developers team for creating this marvelous language and fostering a community around it.

Thanks to Ivo's wife, Christiane, for endless love and encouragement, and to Simon's wife, Angelika, who supported his exploration of new paths.

We hope that this book will be your guide for adding Crystal to your toolbelt and encourage you to start your own Crystal projects!

Happy Crystalling ♥

Ivo Balbaert
ivo.balbaert@gmail.com
Antwerp, Belgium, December 2018

Simon St. Laurent
simonstl@simonstl.com
Varna, New York, December 2018

Part I

Getting Started

Here you will find a solid argument for why you should use Crystal, followed by instructions for setting up a Crystal environment and a mini-tutorial to get you started.

## CHAPTER 1

Diving into Crystal

Crystal promises to be "Fast as C, slick as Ruby." Crystal is an evolutionary change rather than a drastic departure, focusing on clean structures and performance. Crystal, like Ruby, offers a solid object-oriented foundation with functional flavors, and is designed to be approachable to mainstream developers.

In this chapter, you'll see the advantages and benefits of Crystal, including performance benchmarks and a bit of sample code. If you're familiar with object-oriented programming, the code should be easy to understand. This chapter isn't a detailed explanation of the language, however. In later chapters, we'll explore language syntax and semantics in much greater depth.

If you already know you want to work with Crystal, you're welcome to skip ahead. You can save this chapter for a day when you need to convince managers, co-workers, and others that they should be using Crystal, too.

A Programming Language for Humans and Computers

Creator Ary Borenszweig started Crystal in 2011, and was quickly joined by Juan Wajnerman, Brian Cardiff, and the whole team from the Argentinian company Manas Technology Solutions.[1] It's now also carried by a complete open source development on GitHub, with over 250 contributors.

At the time of this writing, Crystal is currently at v 0.27.0. A steady effort to reach the v1.0 production version is ongoing, but a strong and welcoming community already supports Crystal's growing popularity. A Ruby-like compiled language—sounds attractive, right?

It's much easier to program at a lower level in Crystal than it is in Ruby, and Crystal executes much faster. That's why its name contains the letter "C"—a

---

1. http://manas.tech

reference to its native character. In addition to its strong Ruby roots, Crystal also seeks inspiration from other contemporary languages like Rust, Go, C#, Python, Julia, Elixir, Erlang, and Swift. It mixes the best features of its predecessors in a way that no other language does.

Crystal combines the syntax and many idioms from Ruby with:

- A *static type system* where types are mostly *automatically inferred*.
- Automated *garbage collection* that makes the language *memory safe*.
- *Compilation to machine code* through the LLVM toolchain for speed, with emphasis on a low memory footprint.
- A *macro-system* of compile-time evaluation that provides much of the flexibility of Ruby's dynamic approach but with no performance penalty.
- *Full object-orientation*: everything is an object in Crystal.
- Support for *generics* as well as *method and operator overloading*.
- *Scalability and concurrency*, implemented with a cooperative, lightweight, and easier to understand threading model called *fibers*. (Fibers are inspired by the communicating sequential processes, or CSP, architecture that you also see in Go.)

Crystal aims to be *cross platform*, supporting Linux, macOS, and FreeBSD for both x86/64 (64-bit) and x86 (32-bit) architectures. It also has ARMv6/ARMv7 support. Core team members actively work on a Windows port. Crystal is also *self-hosting*: its compiler is written in Crystal itself, making it easier to see how Crystal works. The Crystal name says it all: more transparency. To contribute to the language, all you need to know is the language itself.

Slick As Ruby, But Way Faster

Crystal's unmistakable Ruby flavor brings elegant, readable, and less verbose code. Crystal's "Hello world" example (see hello_world.cr) is brief:

```
puts "Hello, Crystal World!"  # => Hello, Crystal World!
```

which prints a string to standard output. If you want it even shorter, use p, for printing any object:

```
p "Hello, Crystal World!"  # => "Hello, Crystal World!"
```

(If you want to follow along, see *Installing Crystal on Your Machine*, on page 194).

You don't need to put your code inside a class or starting from a main() function. It's just one line!

Crystal is an ideal complement to Ruby: Crystal brings much greater performance in places where Ruby is in need of it, while Ruby can continue to play its highly dynamic role in other parts of an application. To compare performance, let's compare a program that is the same in both Crystal and Ruby, and run it in both contexts.

A Fibonacci number is the sum of its two predecessors, except for 0 and 1, where it returns itself. This program calculates the sum of a series of Fibonacci numbers using a recursive algorithm, and is valid Ruby as well as Crystal code. The program calculates the Fibonacci numbers from 1 to **42** and adds them up in a variable sum, which is shown at the end. The actual calculation happens in the fib method.

```
why_crystal/fibonacci.cr
def fib(n)
  return n if n <= 1
  fib(n - 1) + fib(n - 2)
end

sum = 0
(1..42).each do |i|
  sum += fib(i)
end

puts sum # => 701408732
```

The program is named fibonacci.cr, with .cr as the Crystal extension. (Ruby doesn't mind.) Looking at the code of fibonacci.cr, you'll only see Ruby idioms: variables without type indication, a familiar method definition, and the .each iterator over a range.

We'll time its execution on the same machine: Ubuntu 16.04, 64-bit OS, AMD A8-6419 processor with 12GB of memory. The code isn't highly tuned, but because the same code runs in both languages, it's a fair basic comparison.

Let's see how Ruby performs:

```
$ time ruby fibonacci.cr

real    3m44.437s
user    3m43.848s
sys     0m0.048s
```

Luckily, I went for a coffee. Now here's Crystal in its development mode:

```
$ time crystal fibonacci.cr

real    0m12.149s
user    0m12.044s
sys     0m0.356s
```

Crystal performs the same task in 12s, including the build (compilation) time, a performance improvement of 18.5 times.

If you were going to use this program in a production environment, you'd make a release build:

```
$ crystal build --release fibonacci.cr
```

This generates an executable file called fibonacci, and looking at its execution:

```
$ time ./fibonacci

real    0m10.642s
user    0m10.636s
sys     0m0.000s
```

you'll notice an additional improvement, giving a relative speed improvement of 21 times over Ruby!

Not all Crystal code will run this much faster. But in general, you can expect a dramatic speed boost of 5 to 100 times compared to Ruby, while at the same time consuming much less memory. For other dynamic languages, the gain will be a bit smaller, but it will still be quite significant.

Here[2] is a comparison calculating fibonacci(45) in different languages on faster hardware:

Language	Version	Result(s)
C	gcc 4.9.2	3.575
Crystal	v0.20.1	6.981
Rust	1.14.0	7.808
Julia	v0.5.0	9.657
LuaJIT	2.1.0-beta2	10.150
Go	go1.7.4	10.249
Node.js	v7.3	15.122

Crystal is compiled to native code, yet development speed isn't hindered by that: you can run a project (even when it contains dependencies on other libraries) as simple as this:

```
$ crystal project.cr
```

This looks like an interpreter mode. Nevertheless, the source code was completely compiled to a temporary file containing native code and then executed. Remember: Crystal has no interpreter and no virtual machine.

_____

2. http://blog.seraum.com/crystal-lang-vs-nodejs-vs-golang-vs-julia-vs-rust-vs-luajit-vs-c-fibonacci-benchmark

So what then are the language differences between Ruby and Crystal that explain this huge performance gap? Crystal is compiled into executable code, and in order to do that, the compiler needs to know the types of all expressions in the code. But because it's a smart compiler that figures out most types by itself through an inference algorithm, the compiler rarely requires you to annotate your code with types. However, you're also very welcome to explicitly annotate your code with types to make your intentions clearer to both human readers and the compiler.

Crystal isn't completely compatible with Ruby—it won't run Rails, and it doesn't (yet) have a complete equivalent to irb. But using almost all of Ruby's idioms, it's a close relative, so porting Ruby code to Crystal is quite straight-forward. We've gathered the most relevant porting considerations in Appendix 2, *Porting Ruby Code to Crystal*, on page 205.

Ruby also often offers you a choice between several methods that do exactly the same thing, like length, size, and count for Enumerable types, or map vs. collect and select vs. find_all. Crystal, going all the way for efficiency, adheres to a "single-way approach," preferring size, map, and select in these cases.

Almost As Fast As C

Although language comparison benchmarks shouldn't be regarded as definitive truths, they do give a good relative indication of how a language compares to its peers. Don't just consider execution time and memory usage. Think also about code size in each language (LOC) and complexity.

Unlike Ruby, other dynamic languages, and even Java or C#, Crystal is not interpreted or executed in a virtual machine. Instead, Crystal is compiled to native code ahead of execution using the LLVM[3] toolchain. This approach gives you all of the LLVM optimizations (existing and future) for free. LLVM is a compiler infrastructure project, which makes it easier to write compilers for all sorts of languages and platforms, including Apple's Swift and Mozilla's Rust. Compiled applications are often much easier to distribute because dependencies can be compiled into a single file, and they have a faster startup time.

Let's compare some results[4] for ahead-of-time or JIT (Just-In-Time) compiled languages, first on implementing an artificial Turing-complete programming language in the following table on page 8.

---

3. http://en.wikipedia.org/wiki/LLVM
4. https://github.com/kostya/benchmarks

Language	Time(s)	Memory (Mb)	Lines of code (LOC)
C++	1.94	1.0	101
Rust	2.42	4.8	86
Crystal	2.91	1.2	77
Nim	3.14	0.8	98
Go	4.2	10.0	124
Java	4.03	513.8	136
C# .NET	16.03	16.9	90

You can find many many more results at kostya[5] and the are-we-fast-yet benchmarks,[6] where you can find more comparisons and information. A recent academic study[7] also concluded: "Java on the HotSpot VM reaches the highest peak performance. The second fastest language implementation is Crystal, which uses LLVM as a compiler backend. Performancewise it is close to Java."

You can see how C and Crystal compare directly on benchmarks that were done for both of them:

Benchmark - Time(s)	C	Crystal	Crystal is slower by factor
BinaryTrees	5.08	8.11	1.60
Fannkuchredux	2.83	4.22	1.49
Fasta	2.21	4.84	2.19
Mandelbrot	10.13	10.98	1.08
Meteor	0.06	0.16	2.67
Nbody	1.59	1.93	1.21
Pidigits	0.85	3.72	4.38
Regexdna	2.07	2.15	1.04
Revcomp	0.23	2.19	9.52
Spectralnorm	6.72	6.91	1.03
		Average:	2.62

Crystal's execution speed is reliably within a factor of 1-3 of C/C++, playing in the same first-tier league of languages as Rust, Go, D, or Nim. Crystal often beats some or all of these languages in certain benchmarks. And it does that consistently with the most compact code.

---

5.   https://github.com/kostya/crystal-benchmarks-game

6.   https://github.com/smarr/are-we-fast-yet/tree/master/benchmarks/Crystal

7.   http://stefan-marr.de/papers/dls-marr-et-al-cross-language-compiler-benchmarking-are-we-fast-yet/

Speeding Up the Web

Web frameworks have been a stronghold for dynamic languages like Ruby, Python, and PHP. How does Crystal compare?

The Crystal standard library web server is itself very performant. In a test comparing web servers implemented in Node.js, Nim, Rust, and Scala, the Crystal HTTP::server handled more requests per second[8] than any other server. Tests come and go, but Crystal continues to do well despite being limited to one processor for now.

What about more fully fledged web frameworks? Right now, one framework in Crystal stands out: *Kemal.* This small and flexible web framework supports a RESTful interface, very much like Sinatra in Ruby. For a more complete discussion, see *Build Web Applications with the Kemal and Amber Frameworks,* on page 173. Kemal and Sinatra were compared using wrk, a modern HTTP benchmarking tool for tests using a single core and a web form of the Hello-world app. Here's the Crystal source code:

```
why_crystal/kemal.cr
require "kemal"

get "/" do
  "Hello from Kemal!"
end

Kemal.run
```

Servers built on both frameworks were tested with 100 connections for a duration of 30 seconds:

```
$ wrk -c 100 -d 30 http://localhost:3000
```

The results are shown in the figure on page 10—the y-axis shows the number of processed requests per second.

Another similar benchmark showed Kemal handling up to 64986 requests per second with an average response time of 170μs per request, while Sinatra answered 2274 requests per second with an average time of 43.82ms. Both tests show that Kemal processes around 28x more requests per second than Sinatra. (This is from Serdar Dogruyol's talk at the Poly Conf 2016 conference: "Kemal: Building lightning fast web applications with simplicity.")

---

8.   https://github.com/costajob/app-servers

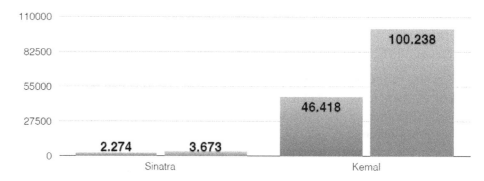

(Higher is better: left = with logging, right = without logging).

What about web frameworks in other languages? Taichiro Suzuki made a similar kind of benchmark[9] in March 2017 by comparing Sinatra, Roda, and Rails (all in Ruby), and Echo (written in Go) with Kemal and router_cr (both Crystal). This showed that Kemal and router_cr both outperform all other frameworks. Serdar Dogruyol made the following benchmark:[10]

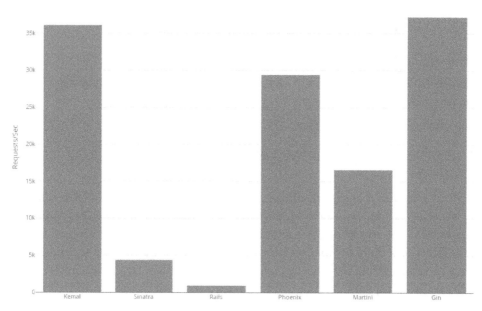

(Higher is better: Sinatra/Rails in Ruby, Phoenix in Elixir, Martini/Gin in Go.)

---

9.   https://github.com/tbrand/which_is_the_fastest
10. https://github.com/sdogruyol/kemal-showdown/pull/5

Considering these results, we can safely conclude that Crystal is an excellent performance choice for web servers and web frameworks.

Talking to Databases

Crystal comes out of the box with a database library to work smoothly with SQLite, MySQL, and PostgreSQL. Stefan Wille[11] compared the performance of a Redis client-library in different languages talking to Redis in a pipelined mode. This means that the client queues up all 1,000,000 requests, sends them in one big batch, and then receives all responses in another batch, which minimizes the impact of the operating system and focuses the measurement on the overhead caused by the client library and by the programming language.

The results, represented in number of commands handled per second, are quite persuasive. (The two "Ruby" entries on the right use different Redis client libraries.)

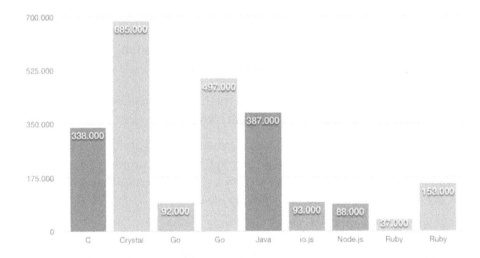

From the evidence you saw in the preceding sections, it will come as no surprise to learn that Crystal can be effectively applied for web servers, heavy-lifting backend server processing, command-line tools, microservices, working with databases, and even games.

Apart from the speed, what other advantages does Crystal bring to the table?

---

11. https://www.stefanwille.com/2015/05/redis-clients-crystal-vs-ruby-vs-c-vs-go/

More Safety Through Types

Crystal provides more than performance. The Crystal compiler also provides the benefits of static type-checking, preventing lots of runtime errors. The following snippet, which again is both Ruby and Crystal syntax, shows how this works. It calls a method add, which in turn calls + on several values:

```
why_crystal/error1.cr
def add(x, y)
  x + y
end

puts add(2, 3) # => 5
# () can be left out in method calls
puts add(1.0, 3.14)             # => 4.14
puts add("Hello ", "Crystal") # => "Hello Crystal"
# + concatenates two strings
```

You know that + is defined for integers, floats, and strings, but what if you try:

```
puts add(42, " times")
```

To run this in Ruby, use $ ruby error1.cr. The program puts out the values 5, 4.14, and "Hello Crystal," and then reports a runtime error crashing the program:

```
'+': String can't be coerced into Fixnum (TypeError).
```

Ruby interprets code when it is run, and methods are looked up at runtime. Ruby won't find the problem until it's well into the program.

To run the same code in Crystal, use $ crystal error1.cr. This time there is no output. Crystal compiles the complete program in a separate step before execution starts. Because Crystal detects an error during that process, it stops at compile time and the program doesn't run:

```
Error in error1.cr:8: instantiating 'add(Int32, String)'
add(42, " times")
    ^~~
in error1.cr:2: no overload matches 'Int32#+' with type String
```

Crystal has no method to add a string to an integer. The compiler knows this and halts. The code never comes close to execution.

Now take a look at this situation, again in code with syntax that fits both Crystal and Ruby:

```
why_crystal/error2.cr
str = "Crystal"
ix = str.index('z')
puts str[ix]
```

This looks up the location ix of the character 'z' in the string str, which contains "Crystal." What if the character doesn't occur in the string as is the case here? In both Ruby and Crystal, ix would be nil to indicate that nothing is found.

Ruby throws an error if the character isn't found: $ ruby error2.cr

```
error2.cr:3:in `[]': no implicit conversion from nil to integer (TypeError)
from error2.cr:3:in `main'
```

This happens at runtime, hopefully while you're testing and not while your customers are using the program.

Crystal, however, gives an error during compilation:

```
$ crystal error2.cr
```

```
Error in error2.cr:3: no overload matches 'String#[]' with type (Int32 | Nil)
```

The error contains a lot more information, but this is the key line. The compiler catches the possible error, even before you're in a testing phase, let alone in production. The error message also pinpoints the exact problem, somewhat better than Ruby does: the [] method of String won't work with a nil argument. In other words: looking up item at position ix of str fails when ix is nil.

You can remedy this situation as in Ruby by testing ix as follows:

```
why_crystal/error2.cr
if ix
  puts str[ix]
end
```

An if in Crystal accepts true and all other values, except false and nil (and null pointers). So in the if-branch Crystal knows that ix can't be nil, and there's no compile error any longer.

Crystal also lets you avoid compilation errors while still supporting methods that accept a variety of different types. Moving beyond Ruby syntax, Crystal lets you create different methods that have the same name but use different argument types, called *overloading*.

No to the Billion-Dollar Mistake

One of the heroes in our field, Tony Hoare, called the introduction of a null-reference in ALGOL W (1965) his "billion-dollar mistake." Since then and up until the present, this error has plagued the software industry, forcing developers to either check every reference in a program or risk disaster.

```
In Ruby: undefined method '...' for nil:NilClass
In JavaScript: undefined is not an object
In Java: java.lang.NullPointerException
In Python: AttributeError: 'NoneType' object has no attribute '...'
In C#: Object reference not set to an instance of an object
In C/C++: segmentation fault
...
```

Nil even caused trouble in the code snippet error2.cr of the previous section. Crystal saves you from this error by not allowing nil (null) pointer exceptions. Although nil is a perfectly valid value, used to represent the absence of a value, the Crystal compiler carefully detects every possible occurrence of nil and prevents every dangerous use of it through a compiler error. It makes you not use any methods on a nil—in other words, it forces you to be nil-safe. Look carefully at the error message in error2.cr in *More Safety Through Types*, on page 12:

```
no overload matches 'String#[]' with type (Int32 | Nil)
```

The compiler detected an expression ix that could either be an integer of type Int32, or nil (of type Nil). At compile-time, this expression is said to be of the union type (Int32 | Nil) (you can read | as or). The index-method [] that's called on ix is only defined for Int32, not for Nil.

Even languages that support types often don't have compiler-based checking for nil. Java and C# programmers, for example, get to write if a lot of times looking for null. While of course you'd never write sloppy code without such checks, and you'd always test your projects exhaustively, Crystal can still spare you typing while saving you some self esteem. The Crystal compiler expects a higher level of quality and thoroughness in your code than Ruby or Java does. It implements almost the same checks as the Rust compiler[12] does, but comparing the syntax, you could call Crystal a "simpler Rust."

In dynamic languages like Ruby or Python, and sometimes in languages executed in a virtual machine like Java and C#, you'd use something like a try/catch statement to prevent a runtime exception. This is a resource-hungry construct when triggered, and it also clutters the code. In Crystal, this exception simply won't happen in runtime. You don't need to create a mess to catch it.

Batteries Included

Crystal comes with a lot of tooling baked in to help you get started quickly on projects. Because the compiler is smart enough to catch many errors,

---

12. https://doc.rust-lang.org/reference/types.html

Crystal has effectively already written many of the input tests you'd need to write when coding in dynamic languages. Nevertheless, the Crystal standard library contains a Spec module supporting unit testing and Behavior-Driven Development. It even has the look and feel of RSpec, the well-known BDD framework in Ruby.

Here's an overview of what's included:

• Project creation tools with ready-made code templates and spec testing.

• Dependency management, which offers easy automated inclusion of external packages (called *shards*: a pun on Crystal and *shared* library).

• A code formatter (format) so that all code is standardized and easily recognizable, avoiding zealous code format discussions.

• A documentation generator (docs) that uses the Markdown format.

• An elegant, local web-based environment for working with code, called the Crystal playground,[13] containing tools for exploring the code, like showing context and types.

The standard library supports modern needs, containing, for example, JSON parsing, Crypto, HTTP clients and servers, Websockets, OAuth2, and database drivers. This is enriched by a whole ecosystem of more than 2200 shards (these are Crystal's libraries or packages), produced by a vibrant community.

Deploying a Crystal app is also super easy: just copy the executable to the target system. No need to install a dedicated runtime, and no problems with Crystal code dependencies.

Putting Crystal to Good Use

Crystal brings C-like performance to general-purpose programming like Ruby, Python, Java, or C#. Here are some of the key areas where Crystal can be applied:

• Fast web apps that look and feel like Ruby
• Fast Ruby extensions
• Backend processing
• Web services and microservices
• Command-line applications
• Data science applications

---

13. http://play.crystal-lang.org/

- Games and graphic renderers
- Small utility programs
- IoT applications

Crystal could play a key role in helping Ruby-based startups take their performance to the next level. If you need to optimize parts of a Ruby project, it makes more sense to port code to Crystal than to C or Go.

Some 15 companies, such as ProTel, Bulutfon, DuoDesign, Appmonit, Rain-Forest QA, and Manas itself, already use it for production projects. Some of them, such as ProTel and Bulutfon, experienced scaling problems with their Ruby server infrastructure. For that reason, they rewrote their web service using the Kemal framework in Crystal. In one instance at ProTel, 100 Unicorn workers could be replaced by a single Kemal process to do the same amount of work.

A Company's Story Crystallized: Red Panthers

P. S. Harisankar is the founder, CEO, and CTI of Red Panthers,[14] which is a Ruby on Rails development studio that builds web and mobile applications. It is based in Cochin, India and Wyoming, USA.

> *Ivo:* *What production projects do you use Crystal for?*
>
> *P. S. Harisankar:* *We have a POS (Point Of Sale) system that reads RFID tags from a reader and displays them on a web page. Then the user commits this data to our cloud server, which marks the sale. The cloud app is built in Ruby on Rails.*
>
> *Ivo:* *Why did you decide to use Crystal for these applications?*
>
> *P. S. Harisankar:* *Our local dashboard for the previous POS system was too slow: delay of seconds during a sale is not acceptable. The client required a better response time at the local readers, so we rewrote it in Crystal and are now able to provide a 10 to 15 micro-second response, a 200,000x improvement!*
>
> *We are a Ruby on Rails firm, and if Crystal hadn't existed, our client was leaning toward C++ or Go since we had also worked in Go before. But using Crystal felt more natural for us as we already have parts of the code written in Ruby. It helped us to easily port these to Crystal.*
>
> *Ivo:* *What types of problems does Crystal solve best?*
>
> *P. S. Harisankar:* *Right now, Crystal is our go-to tool when it comes to building an executable application or doing system programming (managing printers,*

---

14. https://redpanthers.co

readers, process-monitors, and so on), or when our clients ask for API service with micro-second requirement. Being a Ruby on Rails dev shop also helped us to work in Crystal. I can ask anyone on my team to have a go at a Crystal program and they love it.

Ivo: *What was it like to develop with Crystal?*

P. S. Harisankar: *Using the Kemal framework, we were able to build a simple web application, have it compiled down to an executable file, and then run that executable as a service. Our POS system is available on a port, using websockets. All the configurations, can be modified in a config.yml file and then our client/ technician only has to restart the service.*

Coming from a dynamic language environment to a static language had its cost. I had to care about the datatypes that we were using and how we were using them. It did make me think more ahead of time. Because it's a pretty new language, we had problems with finding good blog articles on it, but the gitter chat of both Kemal[15] and Crystal[16] helped us a lot.

Ivo: *Are there any aspects of Crystal that specifically benefit customer satisfaction?*

P. S. Harisankar: *Our client told us that he needs to build a system that can be deployed without the help of a programmer to install all the dependencies, and so on. It should be a drop in, or a deb package. Ruby was out of the question as we would need to install the Ruby VM and set up the server. We were able to package all the contents of this project—the JavaScript, HTML, Bootstrap theme, and so on —inside a single executable, needing only a second file for configuration.*

Ability to compile down our program to one executable was what sold Crystal to us and then to our client. The program running so fast was also a requirement that Crystal satisfied. Not having an Internet connection is not a deal breaker: the system keeps a local record of the sale and item catalog, and synchronizes with the cloud server when it has Internet.

Ivo: *What advantages or disadvantages have you experienced from deploying a Crystal application in production?*

P. S. Harisankar: *The system worked out of the box, and made our POS interface run like silk. We are running Crystal in 18 machines now, and so far we haven't faced issues.*

Ivo: *What do you like the most about Crystal, compared to other languages?*

P. S. Harisankar: *Its speed and WebSocket support in Kemal. For now, Crystal is satisfying our requirements very well.*

---

15. https://gitter.im/sdogruyol/kemal
16. https://gitter.im/crystal-lang/crystal

Wrapping Up

We hope that this brief overview has convinced you of Crystal's potential, and you're ready to dive deeper. Later in the book, you'll see even more Crystal features that add to its popularity, such as the following:

- The capability to use generic types in data structures and methods
- A macro system for generating code
- A lightweight concurrency system with fibers and channels
- Easy C bindings

We'll explore these in detail in subsequent chapters, but first, we'll build ourselves a comfortable Crystal coding environment.

## CHAPTER 2

Crystal Foundations

In this chapter, you'll work through a Crystal tutorial. You'll learn to create and manipulate simple kinds of data and data structures. You'll write code that decides what to do based on the data it receives, and you'll learn how to structure that code into methods, classes, modules, and fibers. This chapter will give you the foundation you need to do simple things in Crystal, and later chapters will provide much more detail about larger possibilities.

If you're a Rubyist, Crystal should make you feel right at home. You can probably skim through, focusing especially on differences from Ruby. In fact, in *Organizing Code in Classes and Modules*, on page 34, you'll port some Ruby code step-by-step to Crystal. You'll soon realize that with Crystal, it's all about the messages you get at compile-time, while with Ruby, everything happens at runtime.

If you're not a Ruby developer, the syntax may seem strange at first, but in time, you'll see how concise and intuitive it is.

Then, in Part II, we'll take a closer look at some important details and gain more insight into why Crystal works the way it does.

Start up your Crystal Playground[1] environment to follow along.

Using Basic Variables and Types

Programming is largely about moving data from place to place, and you'll need containers for that data. Crystal's variables can store different kinds of data. As in most languages, you assign them with the = sign.

---

1. https://play.crystal-lang.org/

```
foundations/variables.cr
name = "Diamond"
element = 'C'
hardness = 10
```

Crystal assignment does more than just put a value into the variable, however. The compiler infers the type of a variable from the value(s) assigned. You can see the variable types the compiler inferred—through type reflection—by testing with the typeof expression.

```
foundations/variables.cr
puts typeof(name)      # => String
puts typeof(element)   # => Char
puts typeof(hardness)  # => Int32
```

Crystal interpreted the name variable as a String because you used double quotes. It interpreted element as a Char (a single character value) because you used single quotes. It interpreted hardness as an integer, specifically a 32-bit integer, because 10 is a short number with no decimal point. (typeof is a great diagnostic tool, but if you're building it into production code, you're working against Crystal's emphasis on managing type details during compilation.)

Most of the time, you can trust Crystal to infer the variable type you want. If you want to be more explicit about it, you can tell the compiler what you want, and the compiler will enforce it for you.

```
foundations/variables.cr
hardness : Int32
hardness = 10
puts typeof(hardness) # => Int32
hardness = "20"  # => Error... type must be Int32, not (Int32 | String)
```

As the first line of that shows, you can declare a variable and its type before assigning it. The Crystal compiler will then use that type in deciding whether later assignments are appropriate. But you can't use that variable for anything before assigning a value to it. (Unless you explicitly define the type of a variable, Crystal will let you assign values of different types to it, and the compiler will keep up if possible.)

You can also declare and assign in the same line, like hardness : Int32 = 10. (Int32 is a signed 32-bit integer, and the spaces around the colon are required.) Remember, however, that you can let Crystal infer variable types most of the time, and you don't need to fill your code with type declarations.

When it's convenient, you can also assign values to multiple variables at one time.

foundations/variables.cr
```
name, element, hardness = "Diamond", 'C', 10
```

If you'd prefer, you can also put multiple statements on one line if you separate them with a semicolon.

foundations/variables.cr
```
name = "Diamond"; element = 'C'; hardness = 10
```

Semicolons enable you to put multiple statements of any kind on a line, not just variable assignments.

If you're in a hurry, you can also switch or swap the values of two variables in one line:

crystal_new/variables.cr
```
# swap
n = 41
m = 42
n, m = m, n
n # => 42
m # => 41
```

(Behind the scenes, Crystal's compiler creates a temporary variable to make this work.)

You may want to create named values that take only one value, called constants. Normal variables, which can change value, start with lowercase letters and use underscores for spaces, called snake or underscore case. Constants, which can't change value, start with uppercase letters, and they're traditionally written in all capitals with underscores for spaces. If you try to set a value for them after they've been set, the Crystal compiler will protest.

foundations/variables.cr
```
DIAMOND_HARDNESS = 10
DIAMOND_HARDNESS = 20  # => already initialized constant DIAMOND_HARDNESS
```

Crystal also includes some starkly limited types that are useful for logical operations. Boolean variables can accept the values of true and false, while nil (of type Nil) explicitly means there is no value.

Not Global

Ruby supports global variables whose names start with $. Crystal's variables are always locally scoped, and it has no global variables.

Variable Operations

Now that you have containers to hold values, you'll want to do things with those values. Crystal offers the traditional mathematical operations, with a few variations depending on whether floats or integers are being processed. (You can mix floats and integers as well.)

```
foundations/operations.cr
d = 10 + 2    # => 12
e = 36 - 12   # => 24
f = 7 * 8     # => 56
g = 37 / 8    # => 4 (integer division)
h = 37 % 8    # => 5 (integers remainder / mod)
i = 36.0 / 8 # => 4.5 (float, or use fdiv function)
```

Strings support the + operator for concatenation that is found in many programming languages.

```
foundations/operations.cr
"this" + "is" + "a" + "test" # => thisisatest
"this " + "is " + "a " + "test" # => this is a test
```

Concatenation works, but it's a clumsy tool. The first item has to be a string for it to work at all, and it'll break if you try to add a number, Ruby style. Fortunately, Crystal lets you assemble strings more naturally with interpolation.

```
foundations/operations.cr
name = "Diamond"
hardness = 10
"The hardness of #{name} is #{hardness}." # => The hardness of Diamond is 10.
```

Crystal evaluates the value of any #{expression} syntax, converts it to a string if necessary, and combines it with the rest of the string.

Underneath these operators is a key truth of Crystal: all of these values are objects. Crystal maps common operator syntax to methods, making it easier for you to write readable code. The type corresponds to a class, which means that all of these values have methods you can use. For example, size is a method on String objects, which returns the number of characters as an Int32.

```
foundations/operations.cr
name = "Diamond"
hardness = 10
name.size     # => 7
hardness.size # => compilation error - undefined method 'size' for Int32
```

But size isn't a method for Int32, so the compiler will give you an "undefined method 'size' on Int32" error.

Your Turn 1

➤ Try out and explain the output of the following statements in Crystal Playground:

```
12 + 12
"12 + 12"
"12" + "12"
"I" * 5
'12' + '12'
5 * "I"
"12" + 12
"2" * "5"
```

Structuring Data with Container Types

Simple variables provide a solid foundation, but as your programs grow, you won't want to keep juggling hundreds of variable names in your head. Crystal provides a number of collection types that let you store a lot of information in structured ways. Arrays and hashes will get you started, and tuples and sets will appear later in the book.

Using Arrays

Sometimes you need to create a list of values, kept in order, and accessible by position. Because this is Crystal, let's collect some minerals. (All of these mineral names are real, and there are lots of them!). The simplest way is to use an array:

```
foundations/compound_types_arrays.cr
minerals = ["alunite", "chromium", "vlasovite"]
typeof(minerals) # => Array(String)

# or, to use a different notation
minerals2 = %w(alunite chromium vlasovite)
typeof(minerals2) # => Array(String)
```

Crystal tells you that minerals isn't just an array; it's an array of String. Its type, Array(String), also contains the type of the items it contains.

You can add minerals easily with the << operator. The size method tells you the number of items it contains:

```
foundations/compound_types_arrays.cr
minerals << "wagnerite"
minerals << "muscovite"
minerals
# => ["alunite", "chromium", "vlasovite", "wagnerite", "muscovite"]
minerals.size # => 5
```

Crystal checks the contents: adding something of another item type isn't allowed. Try adding a number:

foundations/compound_types_arrays.cr
```
minerals << 42
# => Error: no overload matches 'Array(String)#<<' with type Int32
```

You'll get an error while compiling. You'll also get an error if you try to start with an empty array:

foundations/compound_types_arrays.cr
```
precious_minerals = []
# => Error: for empty arrays use '[] of ElementType'
```

This is because the compiler doesn't have enough information to infer its type, and so it can't allocate memory for the array. This is a sharp contrast to Ruby practice, where the type is figured out at runtime. You can create an empty array, but you need to specify a type, either with the [] notation or by creating an object of class Array with new:

foundations/compound_types_arrays.cr
```
precious_minerals = [] of String
precious_minerals2 = Array(String).new
```

As you'd expect, you can read items by index, the position of the item in the array:

foundations/compound_types_arrays.cr
```
minerals[0]  # => "alunite"
minerals[3]  # => "wagnerite"
minerals[-2] # => "wagnerite"
# negative indices count from the end, which is -1
```

You can read subarrays, contiguous sections of arrays, in two different ways. You can give a start index and a size, or use an index range:

foundations/compound_types_arrays.cr
```
minerals[2, 3] # => ["vlasovite", "wagnerite", "muscovite"]
minerals[2..4] # => ["vlasovite", "wagnerite", "muscovite"]
```

What if you use a wrong index? The first item in a Crystal array is always at index 0, and the last at index size - 1. If you try to retrieve something outside of that range, you'll get an error, unlike most Crystal errors, at *runtime*:

foundations/compound_types_arrays.cr
```
minerals[7] # => Runtime error: Index out of bounds (IndexError)
```

If your program logic requires that you sometimes look for keys that don't exist, you can avoid this error. Use the []? method, which returns nil instead of crashing the program:

```
foundations/compound_types_arrays.cr
minerals[7]? # => nil
```

You saw in Chapter 1 that the compiler prevents the use of nil when disaster lurks around the corner. You will soon see how to deal with this in an elegant way.

What if you try to put items of different types in your array?

```
foundations/compound_types_arrays.cr
pseudo_minerals = ["alunite", 'C', 42]
```

This works, but the resulting type of this array is peculiar:

```
foundations/compound_types_arrays.cr
typeof(pseudo_minerals) # => Array(Char | Int32 | String)
```

The compiler infers that the item type is either Char, Int32, or String. In other words, any given item is of the *union type* Char | Int32 | String. (If you want to structure a variable so that it contains specific types at specific positions, you should explore tuples.)

Union types are a powerful feature of Crystal: an expression can have a set of multiple types at compile time, and the compiler meticulously checks that all method calls are allowed for all of these types. You'll encounter more examples of union types and how to use them later in the book.

The includes? method lets you check that a certain item exists in an array.

```
arr = [56, 123, 5, 42, 108]
arr.includes? 42  # => true
```

Need to remove the start or end item? shift and pop can help.

```
p arr.shift # => 56
p arr        # => [123, 5, 42, 108]
p arr.pop    # => 108
p arr        # => [123, 5, 42]
```

If you want to loop through every value in an array, it's best if you do it with the each method or one of its variants.

```
arr.each do |i|
  puts i
end
```

The API for class Array[2] describes many more useful methods. Also, arrays can add and delete items because they are stored in heap memory, and have no

---

2. https://crystal-lang.org/api/master/Array.html

fixed size. If you need raw performance, use a StaticArray, which is a fixed-size array that is allocated on the stack during compilation.

Displaying Arrays

Want to show an array? Here are some quick options:

```
arr = [1, 'a', "Crystal", 3.14]
print arr          # [1, 'a', "Crystal", 3.14] (no newline)
puts arr           # [1, 'a', "Crystal", 3.14]
p arr              # [1, 'a', "Crystal", 3.14]
pp arr             # [1, 'a', "Crystal", 3.14]
p arr.inspect      # "[1, 'a', \"Crystal\", 3.14]"
printf("%s", arr[1])   # a (no newline)
p sprintf("%s", arr[1]) # "a"
```

pp and inspect are useful for debugging. printf and sprintf accept a format string like in C, the latter returning a String.

Your Turn 2

➤ Deleting by value: Most of the time, when you work with arrays, you'll want to manipulate their content based on the positions of items. However, Crystal also lets you manipulate their content based on the values of items. Explore the Crystal API documentation and figure out how to go from ["alunite", "chromium", "vlasovite"] to ["alunite", "vlasovite"] without referencing the positions of the values.

```
minerals = ["alunite", "chromium", "vlasovite"]
minerals.delete("chromium")

p minerals  #=> ["alunite", "vlasovite"]
```

Using Hashes

Arrays are great if you want to retrieve information based on its location in a set, but sometimes you want to retrieve information based on a key value instead. Hashes make that easy.

Let's build a collection that contains minerals and their hardness property using the Mohs Hardness Scale. Given a mineral name, you need to quickly find its hardness. For this, a hash (sometimes called a map or dictionary) is ideal:

```
foundations/compound_types_hashes.cr
mohs = {
  "talc"     => 1,
  "calcite"  => 3,
  "apatite"  => 5,
  "corundum" => 9,
}
typeof(mohs) # => Hash(String, Int32)
```

Its type, Hash(String, Int32), is based on the types of key (String) and value (Int32). You can quickly get the value for a given key using key indexing:

foundations/compound_types_hashes.cr
```
mohs["apatite"] # => 5
```

What if the key doesn't exist, like "gold"? Then, as you saw with arrays, you'll get a runtime error:

foundations/compound_types_hashes.cr
```
mohs["gold"]
# => Runtime error: Missing hash key: "gold" (KeyError)
```

As you saw with arrays, if your logic needs to handle a situation where the key doesn't exist, it's safer to use the []? variant, which returns nil:

foundations/compound_types_hashes.cr
```
mohs["gold"]? # => nil
```

Or, still better, check the existence of the key with has_key?:

foundations/compound_types_hashes.cr
```
mohs.has_key? "gold" # => false
```

Adding a new key-value pair, or changing an existing pair, is easy. You'll use the index notation from arrays, except that you now use the key instead of the index:

foundations/compound_types_hashes.cr
```
mohs["diamond"] = 9  # adding key
mohs["diamond"] = 10 # changing value
mohs
# => {"talc" => 1, "calcite" => 3, "apatite" => 5,
#     "corundum" => 9, "diamond" => 10}
mohs.size # => 5
```

Notice that the size of the hash has increased from 4 to 5. What happens when you add a (key, value) combination where the type of key or value differs from the original items?

foundations/compound_types_hashes.cr
```
mohs['C'] = 4.5 # Error: no overload matches
# 'Hash(String, Int32)#[]=' with types Char, Float64
```

Again, you'll get an error at compile-time: Crystal statically controls your types!

What if you want to start off with an empty hash?

foundations/compound_types_hashes.cr
```
mohs = {}    # Error: Syntax error: for empty hashes use
# '{} of KeyType => ValueType'
```

This doesn't work. Just as with arrays, you need to specify the types again:

foundations/compound_types_hashes.cr
```
mohs = {} of String => Int32 # {}
mohs = Hash(String, Int32).new
```

As you can guess by now, hashes inherit all their methods from the Hash class, which you can find in the API docs.[3]

Your Turn 3

➤ Is that hash empty? Crystal will let you create an empty hash as long as you specify types for both the values and the keys. But empty hashes can create errors and nils when you aren't expecting them. Explore the API docs and find the ways to test for empty hashes and manipulate hashes safely, even when they might be empty.

```
mohs = {
  "talc" => 1,
  "calcite" => 3,
  "apatite" => 5,
  "corundum" => 9
} of String => Int32

p mohs.empty?  => false
```

Controlling the Flow

Now that you have a core set of variables, it's time to drive decisions with them. As with any programming language, Crystal has a number of control flow constructs that let you specify the flow of program execution. We'll go over some of them here, and we'll add some more info in Chapter 3, *Typing Variables and Controlling the Flow*, on page 43.

Making Choices

Crystal offers the classic if expression with variations that let you create complex structures. A simple if expression tests a condition and does something if that condition is met:

foundations/control_flow.cr
```
hardness = 7  # quartz

if hardness < 8
    puts "softer than topaz"
end
# => softer than topaz
```

---

3. https://crystal-lang.org/api/master/Hash.html

In this case, 7 is less than 8, so Crystal will report "softer than topaz." If the value of hardness was 8 or greater, the condition would not have been met, and the if expression would have done nothing.

Crystal also supports more intricate if expressions, adding elsif and else statements to test more conditions in a single location. (For code readability reasons, keep your conditions similar within a single if expression.)

```
foundations/control_flow.cr
hardness = 5.25
if 0 < hardness < 5
  puts "softer than apatite"
elsif hardness < 8
  puts "harder than apatite, softer than topaz"
else
  puts "topaz or harder!"
end
# => harder than apatite, softer than topaz
```

In this case, the first conditional check, on the initial if, failed. The second check, on the elseif, succeeded. The last check, the else, which gets used if none of the other conditions matched, never gets called.

When Crystal evaluates conditions, it calculates whether they are truthy or falsy, not strictly true or false. Crystal takes a fairly constrained view of falsy, treating false and nil (and null pointers) as falsy, and everything else—true, numbers, zero, strings, arrays, you name it—as truthy.

Each branch of an if expression returns a value, so you can combine variable assignment with if to create precise choices.

```
foundations/control_flow.cr
output = if 0 < hardness < 5
           "softer than apatite"
         elsif hardness < 8
           "harder than apatite, softer than topaz"
         else
           "topaz or harder!"
         end
output # => harder than apatite, softer than topaz
```

You can also write the if statement as a suffix, coming at the end of a variable assignment.

```
foundations/control_flow.cr
output = "softer than topaz" if hardness < 8 # => softer than topaz
```

Depending on the condition you're testing, it may be more readable to use unless here:

foundations/control_flow.cr
```
output = "softer than topaz" unless hardness >= 8
output # => softer than topaz
```

While if expressions are readable for simple conditions, they can grow unwieldy quickly. If you want to test the same value against different conditions, the case-when expression can create code that is easier to read.

foundations/control_flow.cr
```
output = case hardness
         when 4
           "hard as fluorite"
         when 7
           "hard as quartz"
         when 10
           "hard as diamond"
         else
           "can't say how hard"
         end # => "can't say how hard"
```

You can also create a case-when expression that uses conditionals much like an if statement.

foundations/control_flow.cr
```
output = case
         when 0 < hardness < 5
           "softer than apatite"
         when hardness < 8
           "harder than apatite, softer than topaz"
         else
           "topaz or harder!"
         end # => harder than apatite, softer than topaz"
```

Looping Around

Sometimes you want to run a block of code a fixed number of times. You can use the times method of the Int type, or you can structure the code block with do ... end if it spreads over multiple lines, or use {...} instead.

foundations/control_flow.cr
```
# Int#times
5.times do
  p "Hi"
  p "Low"
end
# same as:
5.times { p "Hi"; p "Low" }
```

This is simple but speedy: times is as fast as a C loop because it's inlined in the executable code.

Sometimes you want not just to run code a certain number of times but to cover a range of values. You can use Crystal's Range type. You declare ranges with syntax like 2..7, or in general, start..end. The result contains all items from start to end inclusive. (You can use ... for an exclusive range, leaving out the end value.) The start and end values can be integers, characters, or even strings. If you want to inspect the values of a range, you need to convert them to arrays with to_a.

foundations/control_flow.cr
```
inc = 2..7
p inc.to_a  #=> [2, 3, 4, 5, 6, 7]
exc = 2...7
p exc.to_a  #=> [2, 3, 4, 5, 6]
```

Ranges have an each method, which lets you do something with each of the items in succession. This can be useful, for example, to extract a set of values from an array.

foundations/control_flow.cr
```
# Range#each
mohs_list = ["nothing", "talc", "gypsum", "calcite", "fluorite", "apatite",
"orthoclase feldspar", "quartz", "topaz", "corundum", "diamond"]
(2..5).each do |i|
    puts mohs_list[i]
end
# produces:
# gypsum
# calcite
# fluorite
# apatite
```

If you want to process every value in an array, you can skip the range and just use the array's own each method.

foundations/control_flow.cr
```
# Range#each
mohs_list = ["nothing", "talc", "gypsum", "calcite", "fluorite", "apatite",
  "orthoclase feldspar", "quartz", "topaz", "corundum", "diamond"]
mohs_list.each do |mineral|
  puts mineral
end
# produces:
# nothing
# talc
# gypsum
# calcite
```

```
# fluorite
# apatite
# orthoclase feldspar
# quartz
# topaz
# corundum
# diamond
```

If you want to create your own logic for loops, Crystal offers a very basic loop do ... end. This starts an infinite loop, so you have to exit from it with an explicit break:

foundations/control_flow.cr

```
n = 1
loop do
  puts "a mighty crystal"
  n += 1
  break if n == 3
end
# => a mighty crystal
# => a mighty crystal
```

Crystal also implements the typical while construct, which loops until its condition becomes false:

foundations/control_flow.cr

```
a = 1
while (a += 1) < 10
  if a == 3
    next
  elsif a > 6
    break
  end
  puts a
end # => 2, 4, 5 and 6 on successive lines
```

Based on a condition, next goes to the next iteration in the loop, while break exits from the loop. Also, if you're testing that a condition is *not* true, you can make your code easier to read by writing until condition in place of while !condition.

Empty Strings

 Crystal's conventions for character and string literals are more like C than like Ruby, which doesn't have the explicit Chars type for individual characters. Keep in mind that the empty char literal '' doesn't exist in Crystal: if you need an empty string, use "".

Your Turn 4

➤ Write a Crystal program using while and if that correctly puts out the text of this song.[4] As a bonus, try it with the method Int32#downto.

Using Methods

Variables and basic logic provide a foundation, but most code needs more structure than that. Crystal, like Ruby, provides methods as the primary unit of program structure. Methods have names, take arguments (typed arguments in Crystal's case!), and return values. Free-floating methods are also called functions, but because Crystal mostly uses them in the context of objects and classes, you'll mostly hear about methods.

You've already used a few methods—typeof, puts, and p are top-level methods, available anywhere. Some methods are specific to a particular context. The size method is available on strings, while each is on arrays. The methods you've used so far have been built into the core language and library, but you can create your own methods using syntax, def, and end, very much like Ruby's.

```
foundations/methods.cr
def double(num)
  num * 2
end

puts double(6)   # => 12
```

After the name of the method, the arguments are listed in parentheses. This method takes only one argument, but if there were multiple arguments, they would be separated with commas. Arguments are treated as variables within the scope of the method.

Note that a method returns the value of its last expression. The code could explicitly state returns num * 2, but it doesn't have to.

The double method looks like it's meant to work on numbers, with the multiplication operator, but it's actually more flexible than that. Crystal strings also have a multiplication operator. double("6") will return 66. But double(true) will report in line 2: undefined method '*' for Bool.

If you want more control over how your functions respond to arguments of different types, you can specify the type explicitly:

---

4. https://en.wikipedia.org/wiki/99_Bottles_of_Beer

foundations/methods.cr
```
def double(num : Int32)
  num * 2
end

puts double(6)      # => 12
```

Now, if you try to double("6"), Crystal says no, returning a "no overload matches 'double' with type String" error. However, "overload" points to another opportunity. Crystal lets you overload methods, using the same method name with different numbers or types of arguments. If you want to provide different doublings for numbers and strings, you can:

foundations/methods.cr
```
def double(num : Int32)
  num * 2
end

def double(str : String)
  str + " " + str
end

puts double("6")    # => 6 6
puts double(6)      # => 12
```

While you can let Crystal infer types most of the time, there may be moments when you want to specify more precisely.

Your Turn 5

➤ Write a method sample that returns an array with random floating point numbers. The size of the array is passed as an argument to sample. (Hint: Use rand to generate a random float number.)

Organizing Code in Classes and Modules

Variables and methods are powerful, but they need to be organized into larger structures to be very useful. As Crystal is a truly object-oriented language, classes are the main tool for doing that. Classes let you define combinations of methods and associated data, which you can then turn into objects with new. When you've built classes that work with each other, you can organize them into larger modules. Basic Crystal classes look much like Ruby classes, but Crystal makes some changes.

Class Basics

Classes group publicly visible methods and properties, and can have additional methods and variables inside of them to make things work smoothly. Class names start with an uppercase letter, but the rest of the name is typically lowercase or CamelCase, to contrast with variable and method names. When you create a class, you've also defined a new type. This extremely simple example shows defining an empty class, creating an object from it, and checking the type of the object.

foundations/classes.cr
```
class Mineral

end
mine = Mineral.new()
puts typeof(mine) # => Mineral
```

It's not much of an object, but it's easy to add more. When you create a mineral, you should give it a common name and specify its hardness, something like mine = Mineral.new("talc", 1.0). (Hardness isn't necessarily an integer, so this object shifted to floats.) In Crystal, as in Ruby, that means adding an initialize method that takes those arguments.

foundations/classes.cr
```
class Mineral
  def initialize(common_name : String, hardness : Float64)
    @common_name = common_name
    @hardness = hardness
  end
end
mine = Mineral.new("talc", 1.0)
puts typeof(mine) # => Mineral
```

Because the common_name and hardness arguments aren't yet used beyond simple assignment, the compiler lacks the information it needs to determine their type, and will complain if you don't specify them. @common_name and @hardness are instance variables specific to the object created here.

Crystal can also save you some typing on the initialize method. If you use the instance variable names, the ones prefixed with @, as the names of the arguments, Crystal just puts the arguments into the instance variables.

foundations/classes.cr
```
class Mineral
  def initialize(@common_name : String, @hardness : Float64)
  end
end
mine = Mineral.new("talc", 1.0)
puts typeof(mine) # => Mineral
```

But there's currently no way to access those instance variables from outside of the object. If you ask for Mineral.common_name, for example, you'll get undefined method 'common_name' for Mineral.class. You could create a method called common_name= that returns the value of @common_name, but Crystal offers something easier: getters (and setters). To allow reading and manipulation of the common_name outside of the object, and reading of the hardness, you could write:

foundations/classes.cr

```
class Mineral
  getter common_name : String
  setter common_name
  getter hardness : Float64

  def initialize(common_name, hardness)
    @common_name = common_name
    @hardness = hardness
  end
end
mine = Mineral.new("talc", 1.0)
puts mine.common_name # => talc
mine.common_name="gold"
puts mine.common_name # => gold
puts mine.hardness # => 1.0
```

The compiler can find type declarations you specify anywhere in there, but near the top of the class is easy for humans to find, so this set is on the getter. This version lets you read and change the name of the mineral, and read the hardness. If you try to set the hardness, you'll still get an undefined method name error because there is no setter. (If you're a Rubyist, you might have noticed that getter is equivalent to Ruby's attr_reader, setter is equivalent to Ruby's attr_writer, and property is equivalent to attr_accessor. They're just more concise.)

Unlike variables, methods in Crystal classes are visible outside the object by default. They look like the methods you defined earlier but need to be referenced through an object or from inside it. A simple object method would look like:

foundations/classes.cr

```
class Mineral
  getter common_name : String
  setter common_name
  getter hardness : Float64
  getter crystal_struct : String

  def initialize(@common_name, @hardness, @crystal_struct)
  end

  def describe
    "This is #{common_name} with a Mohs hardness of #{hardness}
and a structure of #{crystal_struct}."
  end
end
mine = Mineral.new("talc", 1.0, "monoclinic")
puts mine.describe # => This is talc with a Mohs hardness of 1.0
                   # => and a structure of monoclinic.
```

To give describe something more to do, the example adds a crystal_struct variable. The describe method gathers the three variables of the object and presents them in a sentence. (It also demonstrates that strings can contain line breaks, something that can be useful or annoying depending on your context and preference.)

In Part II, Chapter 5, *Using Classes and Structs*, on page 89, we'll visit classes in depth and will discuss visibility, inheritance, and the class hierarchy.

Your Turn 6

➤ a. Suppose you want to be able to make Mineral objects for minerals for which you don't (yet) know the crystal structure. How could you do this? (Hint: Use a union type for the property.)

➤ b. Add a to_s method that makes a String representation of a Mineral object, and use it in the output. (Hint: The current object is self.)

Making Modules

Modules group methods and classes that implement related functionality. For example, the module Random from the standard library contains methods for generating all sorts of random values. A class can include one or more modules—a so-called *mixin*. That way, the objects of the class can use the methods of the module. Let's make a module called Hardness that contains a method, hardness, to return that value for a given mineral:

foundations/modules.cr
```
module Hardness
  def data
    {"talc" => 1, "calcite" => 3, "apatite" => 5, "corundum" => 9}
  end

  def hardness
    data[self.name]
  end
end
```

In this example, our class Mineral now has only the name property, but it includes the module Hardness:

foundations/modules.cr
```
class Mineral
  include Hardness
  getter name : String

  def initialize(@name)
  end
end
```

By including that module, you can invoke its methods on any `Mineral` object:

```
foundations/modules.cr
min = Mineral.new("corundum")
min.hardness # => 9
```

A class can also extend a module, but then its methods are called on the class.

Executing Code Concurrently Through Fibers

Although they're hard to demonstrate usefully in a tiny example, you should know about Crystal's fibers before going further. They may change the way you structure your programs. In this age of multicore CPUs and distributed computing, developers need their programming language(s) to provide excellent support for concurrency and parallel processing. Unfortunately, this is something Ruby has never been very good at.

In Ruby, you can create multiple threads of execution with `Thread.new`, but they work on the operating system level. You can have a few hundred of them at most. Moreover, in its C implementation, Ruby is limited by the GIL (the Global interpreter lock), which means that only one Ruby thread can work at a time, so only one core is used. In contrast, Crystal is designed from the ground up to support concurrent and parallel computing (though at the time of this writing, parallel support is still in active development).

Crystal's concurrency model is based on two concepts:

1) *Fibers*, which are lightweight threads created by the `spawn` method and controlled by Crystal itself

2) *Channels*, through which fibers communicate with each other

The main program thread is a fiber, but other fibers it spawns will work in the background without blocking main. Channels need to know what kind of data goes through them, so they have to be typed. While versions of Ruby since 1.9 support fibers, the scheduling of Crystal fibers is done by Crystal itself instead of by the programmer.

Here's a simple example that creates a `Channel` for transporting strings. In a loop that repeats 10,000 times, we `spawn` a fiber and tell it to send the string `"fiber #{i}: I like crystals!"` over the channel, so we know which fiber sent it. Then the main fiber receives that string and writes its message to standard output:

```
foundations/fibers.cr
chan = Channel(String).new
num = 10000
num.times do |i|
```

```
  spawn do
    chan.send "fiber #{i}: I like crystals!"
  end
  puts chan.receive
end

# =>
# fiber 0: I like crystals!
# fiber 1: I like crystals!
# fiber 2: I like crystals!
# ...
# fiber 9999: I like crystals!
```

In practice, of course, there is much more to it than that.

Notice an important distinction between "concurrent" and "parallel" in Crystal conversation: *concurrent* means that a number of fibers are running in one thread, so executing on one core, called coroutines in many other languages. *Parallel*, on the other hand, means that two or more code paths are executed at the same time, each on a different core or CPU.

Up to the current version, 0.26.1, Crystal code runs in a single thread. That means it's concurrent, and it does this well and fast, but it doesn't yet run in parallel on several cores. The Crystal core team is actively working to make the language run parallel in the near future.

We'll have a lot more to discuss about this topic in *Creating Concurrent Code*, on page 159.

Your Turn 7

➤ Using this example, time how long it takes to spawn 500,000 fibers.

A Company's Story Crystallized: Dev Demand

Dan Holmes is a developer and business expert from Dev Demand Co.,[5] which is an enterprise startup accelerator, assisting enterprises to innovate within their industry. It is based in Ipswich Queensland, Australia.

> **Ivo:** *What production projects do you use Crystal for?*

> **Dan Holmes:** *We have built an open source command-line project management tool called OM.[6] We're now building a larger commercial product called Notification Engine, which is designed to aggregate notifications from many providers and digest them to email at a speed and frequency that can be customized.*

---

5.   https://devdemand.co/
6.   https://gitlab.com/OpenTrustee/om

Ivo: *Why did you decide to use Crystal for these applications?*

Dan Holmes: *We love the syntax of Ruby but hate its speed. Crystal has the beauty of Ruby syntax and the power of Go. We also considered PHP and Python for our projects, but decided to go with Crystal.*

Ivo: *What kinds of problems does Crystal solve best?*

Dan Holmes: *We see the greatest use for command-line tools, back-end APIs, and scheduled jobs.*

Ivo: *What was it like to develop with Crystal?*

Dan Holmes: *Developing with Crystal is absolutely impressive. It takes very little time to understand and get started with it. It is quick to learn, quick to compile, easy to deploy. Its parity with Ruby is a big help when trying to write code, and most of the common tools you'd need to work with a statically compiled, typed language like Crystal are built in. Some of the tools are better even than the Go tooling.*

Ivo: *Are there any aspects of Crystal that specifically benefit customer satisfaction?*

Dan Holmes: *Customers appreciate mostly the speed and reliability of the application.*

Ivo: *What advantages or disadvantages have you experienced from deploying a Crystal application in production?*

Dan Holmes: *The main advantage to deployment with Crystal is that it's a single binary you can just push. The main disadvantage, however, is that if the platform environment you're using to do the builds doesn't match your production environment, then you're going to have to recompile it on the server. This is an issue easily solved by using something like Docker containers.*

Ivo: *What do you like the most about Crystal, compared to other languages?*

Dan Holmes: *We like that Crystal is fast and typed, and eliminates a lot of common problems you'd see in production with compile-at-runtime languages like Python and PHP. The errors seem to be much more intuitive than in Go as well, which makes debugging a breeze.*

Wrapping Up

Using some simple mineral examples, we explored Crystal's basic constructs and syntax. You got to see the basic types, you learned how to repeat code and control program flow, and you explored some collection types like arrays and hashes. You also learned how to work with methods, classes, and modules, and you converted a Ruby example to Crystal. We finished up with a simple example of how to use fibers. Along the way, you got to see how the compiler guides you toward more robust and safe code.

In Part II, you'll get much more detail on all of those topics, and see how Crystal combined its design decisions to emphasize performance.

Part II

Building Blocks

In this part, we'll go through an overview of the building blocks of Crystal: the why and how of typing in Crystal, basic and compound data types, control structures, methods, classes, modules, generating docs, testing framework, and formatting.

## CHAPTER 3

Typing Variables and Controlling the Flow

Now that you know what Crystal looks like, and you've seen how the compiler behaves, it's time to dig deeper into how Crystal uses types and how they affect the flow of your programs.

Programs manipulate data. That data comes in types, like integer, string, or array. In a dynamically typed language such as Ruby or Python, types are generally not specified in the code. At runtime, when the program executes, the environment determines the types of its data. Crystal rejects this model, largely because it lets errors surface while the program is running. Instead, Crystal compiles the program before it is run, and the compiler needs to know all the types. This lets the compiler signal many possible errors and generate much more optimized code. After the compiler has done its work, the program executes in a much safer and performant way.

However, you won't see that many types written explicitly in Crystal code because the smart compiler can deduce many types. Occasionally, you have to specify the type to help the compiler, such as for the type of the contents of an array.

Crystal also supports more complicated scenarios. In some cases, the compiler concludes that a variable is supposed to contain data of more than one type: for example, sometimes a Boolean, sometimes an integer. Then its type is a *union type*, in this case a Bool | Int32.

In this chapter, we'll dig deeper into types and control flow, and the exception handling that builds on them. To illustrate this, we'll go over how to get input from the terminal. It's not that fancy, but through it, you'll start to get a feeling for how Crystal works.

You'll also gain more experience using specific methods for manipulating strings, arrays, and hashes. The last two are *generic types*: they can hold elements of different types. Then you'll use symbols, enums, and regular expressions and learn some nice tricks in advanced control flow. Throughout this and the following chapters, you'll also start building on the currency converter project, applying many of the things you've learned.

Converting Data Between Types

Most of the time, you don't have to declare types in Crystal, which can be a relief. Sometimes, though, you'll need to make certain that you're working with values of a certain type. You shouldn't count much on Ruby-style automatic conversions: Crystal isn't only *strongly typed*—it wants you to be very careful with conversions. Type conversion is something you'll need to do explicitly in order to satisfy the Crystal compiler. (Though Crystal will deal with the simplest conversions, such as int8 to int32 automatically.)

Money provides a good example: currency rates are numbers with many digits after the decimal point, as in 1 USD is worth 64.34603985 Indian Rupees (INR) today. Although banks don't use floating-point numbers for reasons of precision, they'll work well for an example. Everything we type on a screen arrives in our program as a string, though. Adding numbers is quite different from doing the same with strings, and multiplying strings would be even stranger.

Consider the following, where you try to convert a string representing a currency rate into an integer with the to_i method:

```
"64.34603985".to_i # Runtime error: Invalid Int32: 64.34603985 (ArgumentError)
```

Ruby would happily return the value 64, but Crystal chokes on it at runtime. Crystal is more particular about the conversions it will do because different types have different to_ methods available. You can, for example, convert a string to a float:

```
"64.34603985".to_f # => 64.34603985
```

You can also convert a float into an integer with to_i, but it's going to get truncated without warning:

```
rate = 64.34603985
rate.to_i          # => 64
```

How would you solve this compiler error?

```
rate1 = 64.34603985
rate2 = "7"
rate1 + rate2 # Error: no overload matches 'Float64#+' with type String
```

If you want to add here, you should use to_i on rate2. to_s converts everything into a String, resulting in rate1 and rate2 being concatenated to each other. It makes the compiler happy but probably isn't what you want:

```
rate1 + rate2.to_i  # => 71.34603985
rate1.to_s + rate2  # => "64.346039857"
```

If, instead, you need to make sure you're working with floating point numbers, you'll use to_f:

```
rate1.to_f   # => 64.34603985
rate2.to_f   # => 7.0
```

Of course, there are times when conversions can't work because the data doesn't fit:

```
curr = "Crystal"
curr.to_i  # => Runtime error: Invalid Int32: Crystal (ArgumentError)
```

Crystal also offers more approaches for telling the compiler how you want it to handle types. When the compiler thinks a piece of data has a union type (A|B), but you're sure that it's of a particular type B, you can use as(B) to force the compiler to treat it as type B. Although it sure looks like it, this isn't a conversion like the to_ methods above. Later in this chapter, in *Controlling the Flow and Types*, on page 64, you'll see how to test on a type of a variable, executing different code depending on the outcome.

Your Turn 1

➤ Type conversion among integer types: Crystal is extremely precise about types, but so far you've only used to_i to convert numbers to integers. Crystal offers many different types of integers, though, from 8-bit to 64-bit, both signed and unsigned. How do you convert among those types?

It turns out that you don't have to make the conversions explicit, but there are some tricky bits involving order. The Crystal compiler lets you mix integer types, but the result will default to the type of the first value used, not the largest value used. What do you think will be the results of the following:

```
p int8 = 1_i8   # 8-bit signed integer
p int16 = 16_i16 # 16-bit signed integer
p int32 = 132_i32 # 32-bit signed integer
p int64 = 164_i64 # 64-bit signed integer
p uns64 = 264_u64 # 64-bit unsigned integer

p int64 + int32 + uns64

p int8 + int64
```

Getting Input

You can make bad choices with data while you're programming, but it's even more likely that users will put incorrect data into your programs when asked for input. Creating resilient code means taking special care with user input. In the following section, your program reads input, and you'll learn to make it withstand runtime errors.

To gain a better understanding of how Crystal works with types, let's build a program to read in currencies and their relative exchange rates. Let's start with reading in integer numbers into an array. You can find the complete source code in getting_input.cr.

The console lets you collect input, but the Playground doesn't. To make this work, you have to open up a terminal and type: crystal getting_input.cr.

The user provides the numbers, and you expect that they will be smaller than 256, so they're of type Int8.

```
puts "Enter the numbers one by one, and end with an empty line:"
arr = [] of Int8
```

You'll start with an empty array so you have to indicate the type [] of Int8. There are other ways to indicate the type of the contents of an array, like providing data when you initialize the array:

```
arr1 = [75, 42, 126]
typeof(arr1) # => Array(Int32)
```

Why did the type come up as Int32 when all of those numbers are below 127? Int32 is the default integer type. If you want to force Int8, perhaps for performance reasons, you have to write that explicitly, like so:

```
arr1 = [75_i8, 42_i8, 126_i8]
typeof(arr1) # => Array(Int8)
```

(Crystal offers i8, i16, i32, and i64 suffixes for signed integers, and u8, u16, u32, and u64 for unsigned integers.)

You read from the console with gets, which return everything it reads in as a String. You can display the input with string interpolation.

```
puts "Enter a number:"
num = gets
p "You entered #{num}" # => "You entered 42"
```

Let's add the number to our array:

```
arr << num
```

Crystal won't let you do this:

```
Error: no overload matches 'Array(Int8)#<<' with type (String | Nil).
```

By now, this should be getting familiar. The best way to find out what went wrong is to examine the type of num (first comment out the previous faulty line). You can do this in two ways:

```
p typeof(num) # => (String | Nil)
p num.class   # => String
```

You see that Crystal distinguishes between:

- The *compile-time* type: which is the type the compiler sees, given by typeof
- The *run-time* type: which is the type the object has while the program is running, given by its class

nil can't be appended to an array of integers. But why does the compiler think the input could be nil? Well, instead of entering a number, enter CTRL+D and see what happens: The class of num is Nil! The method << can't be applied to nil. You have to guard against that input. There are several ways to do this. Because nil is falsy, the simplest is to test with if:

```
if num
  arr << num
end
```

We aren't finished yet because now we get another error:

```
no overload matches 'Array(Int8)#<<' with type String.
```

The compiler now knows that num is a String, but the array can only contain Int8. Time to convert the input with to_i8:

```
if num
  arr << num.to_i8
  p arr # => for example: [42]
end
```

Now, Crystal will convert the string to an 8-bit signed integer.

Even if the string is a number, a few things can happen along the way. Including a decimal point will cause an error, as will integers outside of the range of -127 to 128. Non-numeric characters will break this conversion, which you'll address later in the chapter.

Also, the if works for one input. We don't know how many numbers will be provided, so we need a loop. while fits perfectly: gets itself returns a value that can be tested as the while condition. If this value isn't nil or false, while is okay with it and adds it to the array.

```
while num = gets
  arr << num.to_i8
  p arr # => for example: [2, 3, 3, 5]
end
```

Remember: Only nil, false, or null pointers are considered false by Crystal in any logical value or if, unless, while, and until expression. Any other value—including the string "false" and the number 0—works as true while testing expressions.

Assign Shortcut

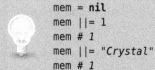

Because of the rules on falsiness, a ||= b, which is a shortcut for a || (a = b), is used to assign b to a only when a is nil:

```
mem = nil
mem ||= 1
mem # 1
mem ||= "Crystal"
mem # 1
```

This is commonly used in memoization: return the value of a when a is not nil, but otherwise return b.

Returning to our input, let's remove any whitespace characters with strip, just in case. To end the loop, test whether the user enters "stop" or just ENTER, and then break from the loop:

```
while num = gets
  num = num.strip  # removes whitespace
  if num == "" || num == "stop"
    break
  end
  arr << num.to_i8
end
p arr # => for example: [78_i8, 56_i8, 12_i8]
```

---

read_line

If testing after gets that the input isn't nil doesn't seem elegant, you can use the read_line method instead.

Try it out—the exercise read_line.cr shows you how to do this.

Putting It Together—Converting Currencies 1

Let's apply all this to a running project. Our goal is to choose a base currency and then roughly convert amounts in other currencies to that base, like: 42 US Dollars (USD) = 277.86846192 Chinese Yuan (CNY). What are the types here? Currency codes such as "CNY" or "USD" are obviously Strings. So are their full names, like "Chinese Yuan". To keep the code and the name together, we could use a Hash(String, String) like this:

```
CURRENCIES = {
  "EUR" => "Euro",
  "CAD" => "Canadian Dollar",
  "CNY" => "Chinese Yuan"
}
```

Store your base currency in a variable base. Conversion rates are decimal numbers. For this example, but not in bank production code, let's use type Float64. So the data structure rates, which contains other currencies and their exchange rates, compared to the base currency, would be a Hash(String, Float64). We read in our base currency (let's default that to "USD"), and then each line brings in another currency and its exchange rate. Here is a first approach:

```
types_and_control_flow/curr_conv1.cr
    puts "Enter the base currency, default is: USD"
    base = gets
①   exit unless base
    if base.strip == ""
      base = "USD" # take "USD" as default value
    end
    puts "Enter the other currencies and their exchange rate,"
    puts "like this: EUR - 0.84320536"
    puts "Stop input by entering 'stop'"
    rates = Hash(String, Float64).new
    while input = gets
②     break unless input
      input = input.strip
      if input == "" || input == "stop"
        puts "No more input: ok, we stop"
        break
      end
③     if !input.includes?(" - ")
        puts("Wrong input format, use: CUR - 1.23456")
        break
      end
④     arr = input.split(" - ")
      curr = arr[0].upcase
      if curr.size != 3
        puts "Currency code must be 3 characters"
        break
      end
      rate = arr[1]
⑤     rates[curr] = rate.to_f
    end
    puts "base: #{base}"
    puts "rates: #{rates}"
```

which will generate a typical output like this:

```
‹  Enter the base currency, default is: USD
⇒  CAD
‹  Enter the other currencies and their exchange rate, like this:
   EUR - 0.84320536
   Stop input by entering 'stop'
⇒  EUR - 0.84
⇒  INR - 64.34
⇒  stop
‹  No more input: ok, we stop
   base: "CAD"
   rates: {"EUR" => 0.84, "INR" => 64.34}
```

❶ Here we test that base is not nil because the compiler requires us to test that. If we don't, we get a compiler error: undefined method strip for Nil in the following line.

❷ We break out from the loop if we don't have any input.

❸ Test the input format. Does it contain a -?

❹ Split returns an array, with the currency code as the first item, and the rate as the second. Now is the time to test the input, like its size (3) or whether the code contains only letters. Try this yourself: use the each_char method of String and the ascii_letter? method of Char. Note that we break out of the loop when in error.

❺ Here we assign the rate to its currency in the Hash. We could also use the shortcut ||=; then only the first input rate will be retained. rate is a String, but rates wants to store this as a Float64, so a conversion is required by the compiler. Leave to_f out and you get: no overload matches 'Hash(String, Float64)#[]=' with types String, String

Test what happens if you enter a rate that isn't a number.

Exception Handling for Faulty Input

It's great to gather outside input for your program, but sometimes that input can create new challenges. You probably know the slogan "Garbage in, garbage out": wrong input can corrupt all further processing. In our previous example, suppose the user enters a string such as "abc" when the program expects an integer number—a string that isn't convertible to an integer. What happens then? Something awful: a runtime error or exception. As a professional programmer, you'll want to avoid this at all costs.

```
‹  Invalid Int8: abc (ArgumentError)
   0x451477: *CallStack::unwind:Array(Pointer(Void)) at ??
```

```
0x465a92: to_i8 at /opt/crystal/src/string.cr 358:5
...
```

You must always guard against dangerous input. The best way to handle this is to do a simple test to_i8? to see whether the string starts with a valid number. If not, it returns nil:

```
if num.to_i8?
  arr << num.to_i8
else
  puts "Input is not an integer."
end
```

Now you'll get a nice error message and no runtime exception! (As in Ruby, Crystal has the convention that methods with names ending in ? will return nil if nothing is found.) If the fault condition is so bad that you want to stop the program with your own error message, use raise:

```
if num.to_i8?
  arr << num.to_i8
else
  raise "Input is not an integer."
end
```

Applying this technique to our currency converter gives us the following:

types_and_control_flow/curr_conv2.cr
```
if rate.to_f?
  rates[curr] = rate.to_f
else
  puts "rate is no decimal number"
end
```

Using a simple puts doesn't stop the program. An alternative is to use the exception handling mechanism begin-rescue:

types_and_control_flow/getting_input_exception.cr
```
puts "Enter the numbers one by one, and end with an empty line:"
arr = [] of Int8
while number = gets
  number = number.strip # removes leading or trailing whitespace
  if number == "" || number == "stop"
    break
  end
  begin
    arr << number.to_i8
  rescue
    puts "integer bigger than 255"
  end
end
p arr # => for example: [78, 56, 12]
```

The rescue-part catches the exception so that the program doesn't crash. Executing an exception handler like this involves allocating memory, and it's generally slow, as in Java or Ruby. You're better off trying to avoid that with simple tests like to_i? or to_f? above, if possible. If you really need to use begin-rescue, minimize the amount of code between begin and rescue to avoid both extra memory usage and potentially complicated logic. Use exceptions only for exceptional things, not for expected things!

As in Ruby, this mechanism can also have an else and an ensure branch. And in rescue, you can use the exception object ex:

```
begin
  # some dangerous code here
  # possibly your own raise "..."
rescue ex
  # execute if an exception is raised
  p ex.message
else
  # execute if an exception isn't raised
ensure
  # this will always be executed
  puts "Cleanup..."
end
```

Chaining Methods

I know you like beautiful code—otherwise you wouldn't be reading this book. Data conversion often requires a predictable sequence of methods. One of the nice things about Crystal is that you can chain methods to create more readable code. A method can be called on any object on which it's defined, and that object can be the result of another method call. Take a look at the following examples:

```
types_and_control_flow/chaining.cr
result = (42..47).to_a                          # => [42, 43, 44, 45, 46, 47]
          .sort { |n, m| m <=> n }              # => [47, 46, 45, 44, 43, 42]
          .reject { |n| n.odd? }                # => [46, 44, 42]
          .map { |n| n * n }                    # => [2116, 1936, 1764]
          .select { |n| n % 4 == 0 }            # => [2116, 1936, 1764]
          .tap { |arr| puts "#{arr.inspect}" }  # => [2116, 1936, 1764]
          .sort!                                # => [1764, 1936, 2116]
          .any? { |num| num > 2000 }            # => true
```

❶ A range is converted to an array with to_a.

❷ The array is sorted in reverse order (<=> is the comparison operator).

❸ All odd numbers are eliminated with reject.

❹ The map function takes another function as argument to square all items.

❺ All numbers divisible by 4 are selected.

❻ tap passes the object to the block and returns it—useful for debugging or compacting code

❼ The array sorts itself.

❽ Check with any? whether it contains a number bigger than 2000.

You also have reduce at your disposal, which accumulates the result of running a calculation on the items of a collection, in the following case the sum of all numbers of the array arr:

```
types_and_control_flow/chaining.cr
sum = (42..47).to_a
              .reduce(0) { |sum, num| sum + num }
              # => 267 (= 42 + 43 +... + 47)
```

The reduce approach brings a functional approach to Crystal calculations.

You can name your methods the same way you would in Ruby:

- Methods that end in a ! (like sort!) by convention change the object on which they are called. (Usually - pp! shows a fuller expression than pp.)

- Methods that end in a ? (such as any?) ask a logical question and return true or false.

Getting Input from Command-Line Arguments

Input isn't always interactive. The rapid start-up of compiled Crystal code makes it an excellent fit for command-line applications. What if you need to supply the program with data or options from the command line?

For example, let's read in two currencies and their relative rate (1 USD = 0.8432053 EUR today): $ crystal argv.cr USD EUR 0.84320536

Crystal, like Ruby, has the top-level ARGV structure to handle this:

```
types_and_control_flow/argv.cr
puts "Number of command line arguments: #{ARGV.size}" # => (1)
ARGV.each_with_index do |arg, i|
  puts "Argument #{i}: #{arg}" # => (2)
end
p ARGV                                   # => (3)
p "Executable name: #{PROGRAM_NAME}"   # => (4)
p "Path to source file: #{__FILE__}"   # => (5)
p "Folder of source file: #{__DIR__}" # => (6)
```

```
# (1) Number of command line arguments: 3
# (2)
# Argument 0: USD
# Argument 1: EUR
# Argument 2: 0.84320536
# # (3) ["USD", "EUR", "0.84320536"]
# (4) "Executable name: /$HOME/.cache/crystal/crystal-run-argv.tmp"
# or (4) "Executable name: ./argv"
# (5) "Path to source file:
#   /$HOME/crystal/Book/code/types_and_control_flow/argv.cr"
# (6) "Folder of source file:
# /$HOME/crystal/Book/code/types_and_control_flow"
```

You can run through ARGV as an array with each or each_with_index and use the do-block for whatever you want to do with the arguments. Here's a more realistic example: if you start up a program, db_json, like this: $ ./db_json sqlite3://db/sqlite3.db, then ARGV[0] contains the database connection string.

Your code has access to the executable name as the constant PROGRAM_NAME. This is "./argv" if you generated an executable with $ crystal build program.cr. When you start it like $ crystal program.cr , you'll see that the executable is created in a special .cache/crystal folder. Here, all compiler intermediary files (such as macro expansions, linker .o files, temporary files from the playground, and so on) are saved.

__FILE__ and __DIR__

 __FILE__ is a special constant that contains the complete path to the current file name. __DIR__ contains the directory of the current file.

Here's a version of our currency converter that reads in the base currency from the command line when starting the program like $ ./curr_conv3 EUR:

```
types_and_control_flow/curr_conv3.cr
base = ARGV[0]?
base = "USD" unless base
```

Using String Methods

Your inputs have arrived as strings, and most kinds of data can be represented as strings. Working with strings is the bread and butter of every programmer. Like Ruby, Crystal is well equipped for string processing. You've been using strings throughout this book, but there are more ways to create strings and more ways to work with them.

Crystal, like Ruby, supports multi-line strings:

```
str = "What a beautiful mineral!"
str1 = "What a
beautiful mineral!" # multi-line string
```

Crystal also supports the use of the backslash to escape characters inside of strings. If you wanted to create the same str1 shown above while keeping it on one line in your code, you could instead type the following:

```
str = "What a beautiful mineral!"
str1 = "What a \nbeautiful mineral!" # multi-line string
```

Typically, you'll want to escape the double quote (\") and the backslash itself (\\). You can also use numeric escaping. \u followed by a hexadecimal number enables you to specify a Unicode character. For example, \u2603 gets you a Unicode snowman.

Once you have strings, Crystal offers you many ways to process them:

```
types_and_control_flow/strings.cr
curr1 = "US Dollar"
curr1[2..4]                          # => " Do"
curr1.reverse                        # => "ralloD SU"
curr1.size                           # => 9    # length or len do not exist
curr1.upcase                         # => "US DOLLAR"
curr1.capitalize                     # => "Us dollar"
curr1.includes? "la"                 # => true
curr1.count "l"                      # => 2
curr1.starts_with? "Us"              # => false # case sensitive!
curr1.ends_with? "ar"                # => true
curr1.index("a")                     # => 7
curr1.sub("ll", "l")                 # => "US Dolar"
curr1.gsub(/([aeiou])/, "*\\1*")   # => "US D*o*ll*a*r"
curr2 = curr1.split("")              # => ["U","S"," ","D","o","l","l","a","r"]
curr2.join("-")                      # => "U-S- -D-o-l-l-a-r"
```

split and join are classics: split transforms a string into an array—we used it in our currency converter—while join goes the other way around, transforming an array into a string.

Strings are created on the heap. They're immutable, which means you can't change their content directly:

```
s = "USD"
s[2] = 's' # => Error: undefined method '[]=' for String
```

For efficiency, you should avoid creating extra strings. In the following snippet, both to_s, +, and string interpolation create a string on the heap, though interpolation is faster:

```
rate = 0.84320536
p "rate: " + rate.to_s # => "rate: 0.84320536"
# string interpolation is more efficient:
p "rate:  #{rate}" # => "rate:  0.84320536"
```

You can also use a String builder and the << method:

```
str = String.build do |io|
  io << "rate: " << rate
end
p str # => "rate:  0.84320536"
```

As your projects grow more complex, efficient string handling will matter even more.

Your Turn 2

➤ a. Split the following string of mineral names into an array where all of the names are uppercase: gold;topaz;apatite;wolframite;calcite;diamond (Hint: Use the map method you learned about in *Chaining Methods*, on page 52).

➤ b. Strings are sequences of UTF8-encoded characters. If you're a cat lover, you might say "hi 猫". Iterate over this string and print each character, code-point, and byte respectively. Consult the docs[1] for available methods. What's the unicode codepoint for the Chinese character for cat, and how many bytes does this character take?

Use "each" Methods For Performance

 Use the each methods for iteration: They're much faster than a simple while loop or looping over a string by indexing with [].

➤ c. object_id

Show that two constant strings with the same value reference the same object on the heap. (Hint: Use the object_id method.) Why would Crystal implement it this way? In general, when two objects have the same object_id, the operator == will return true, as will the method same?. What happens when you ask for the object_id of an integer or a Boolean?

---

1. https://crystal-lang.org/api/master/String.html

Using Symbols as Identifiers

The strings you've been using in this chapter are flexible, but that flexibility imposes performance costs. Suppose you need to sift through a huge file with millions of mineral objects and give each their mineral name, essentially assigning an identifier. You'd be better off using Symbols here, because every instance of a given Symbol is exactly the same object:

```
types_and_control_flow/symbols.cr
class Mineral
  property name

  def initialize(@name : Symbol)
  end
end

mineral1 = Mineral.new(:talc)
mineral8547 = Mineral.new(:talc)

p mineral1.name
# => :talc
p mineral8547.name # => :talc
p :talc            # => :talc

mineral8547.name = :gold
:gold.class # => Symbol
```

Because a Symbol is stored as a unique Int32 value, using them saves memory compared to using strings. Symbols are also an excellent choice for hash keys, instead of using Strings.

Here's how we could use them in our conversion project:

```
types_and_control_flow/curr_conv3.cr
CURRENCIES = {
  :EUR => "Euro",
  :CAD => "Canadian Dollar",
  :CNY => "Chinese Yuan",
  :INR => "Indian Rupee",
  :MXN => "Mexican Peso",
}
```

To convey more meaning, a Symbol's name can also end in ? or ! All operators also have their own Symbol, like :* and :&

```
types_and_control_flow/symbols.cr
ask = :ask1?
call = :call!
op1 = :*
```

Your Turn 3

➤ Is a symbol the same object as a string with the same value?

Using Enums

Sometimes you want to limit options not just to symbols but to a smaller set of possibilities. It can be handy to group variables with a discrete number of values, like the colors of a traffic light or the compass directions, into a specific type. Crystal supports Enums to group related values, specifically when the number of distinct values isn't too big:

```
types_and_control_flow/enums.cr
enum Direction
  North # value 0
  East  # value 1
  South # value 2
  West  # value 3
end

Direction::South       # South
Direction::South.value # => 2
```

Enums are stored internally as integers, but showing their names in the code makes them more readable to humans. In the grand scheme of Crystal things, all enums inherit from the base class Enum, and you can even define methods for them.

Enums have another important advantage: The compiler checks them. But if you misspell a symbol, it's stored as a new symbol.

```
Direction::Eest # Error: undefined constant Direction::Eest
:gold
:goold
```

The extra compiler support gives enums advantages in places where you would have used symbols in Ruby.

Using Regular Expressions

Sometimes you want the flexibility of strings, but you need to process them efficiently. Searching and replacing inside of strings can also use a lot of processing cycles. Regular expressions, or regexes, can reduce the costs of string processing substantially thanks to highly optimized processing models. Crystal uses the PCRE syntax.[2] This is implemented as a C binding to the PCRE C-library. (Though Ruby uses a different regex engine, it also uses PCRE syntax.)

---

2.   https://en.wikipedia.org/wiki/Regular_expression

Patterns are usually created with the /pattern/ literal syntax. If you have a regex that includes a slash you don't want to have to escape, you can also create a pattern with %r(pattern). Once you have a pattern, you can apply it to strings. Use =~ or the match method to check whether two strings match and from which starting position.

```
types_and_control_flow/regex.cr
str = "carbonantimonygolddiamond"
pattern = /gold/
p str =~ pattern # => 14
```

In this case, gold appeared at starting position 14. If gold wasn't in the string, the match would have returned nil. Because nil is falsy, this makes it easy to test for matches with if materials =~ pattern, doing some tasks if there is a match and others if there isn't a match.

You can also extract more information about the string and its relationship to your regex:

```
types_and_control_flow/regex.cr
materials = "carbonantimonygolddiamond"
pat = /(.+)gold(.+)/  # searches for gold

str = "carbonantimonygolddiamond"
str =~ pat # => 0
$1          # => "carbonantimony"
$2          # => "diamond"

str.match pat # =>
# <Regex::MatchData "carbonantimonygolddiamond"
# 1:"carbonantimony" 2:"diamond">
```

In this example, the starting position is reported as 0 (also truthy, which is useful for if) because we allowed for a prefix with (.+). The methods from the Regex class let you look deeper into the match results.

Crystal lets you use string interpolation syntax (#{}) in regular expression literals, giving you potentially powerful opportunities at runtime. This also, of course, lets you create runtime exceptions if you interpolate bad syntax, so be careful!

Putting It Together—Converting Currencies 2

Later on in our project we'll have to fetch daily exchange rates from XML files stored on a website. They contain that information in the following form:

```
<title>1 USD = 0.74402487 GBP</title>
```

At this point in our program, we know the base currency, "USD," and the exchange currency, "GBP," and we want to get the exchange rate 0.74402487. Here's how we can do this:

```
types_and_control_flow/curr_conv4.cr
base_currency = "USD"
currency = "GBP"
line = "<title>1 USD = 0.74402487 GBP</title>" # exchange rate format

regex = {
  :open => /<title>1 #{base_currency} = /,
  :close => / #{currency}<\/title>/
}

rate = line.gsub(regex[:open], "").gsub(regex[:close], "").to_f
                                                    # => 0.74402487
```

The regex pattern /<title\>1 #{base_currency} = / allows us to match with the part before the rate number. In the same way, the pattern / #{currency}<\/title\>/ matches the closing part. Using chained gsub methods, these patterns are erased so that only the rate string is left over, with to_f finishing it off.

Beyond Hashes and Arrays: More Composite Types

Composite types, like the arrays and hashes we met in the previous chapter, make it easier to create more complex applications. Crystal offers more options, like tuples and sets, to address other data models.

Tuples group related values of possibly different types. You can create them with values inside { }, or with Tuple.new:

```
tpl = {42, "silver", 'C'}
tpl.class # => Tuple(Int32, String, Char)
a = Tuple.new(42, "silver", 'C')
```

In case you're wondering how multiple assignments, such as n, m = 42, 43, work, they use tuples. You can access items of a tuple by index:

```
tpl[0]    # => 42        (Int32)
tpl[1]    # => "silver" (String)
tpl[2]    # => 'C'       (Char)
var = 89
tpl[var] # => Index out of bounds (IndexError)
tpl[var]? # => nil
```

The index is checked and, if it's wrong, it generates an error at compile time if literals are involved, but otherwise a runtime IndexError. As with arrays, it's safer to use the []? method, which returns nil in this case. You can use all methods from class Tuple, such as size, each, includes?, map, and so on. Because tuples are created on the stack, they're lighter than arrays, which are allocated on the heap, especially when used inside loops.

Using the shortcut ||= syntax we introduced earlier in *Getting Input*, on page 46 offers a great way to add data pairs:

```
h = {1 => 'A'}
h[3] ||= 'C'
h # => {1 => 'A', 3 => 'C'}
```

We could have used that form in our conversion project like this:

```
rates[curr] ||= rate.to_f
```

This means that the exchange rate is set only to the first value; subsequent values would not change it.

If you want more meaning in your data structure, Crystal also has *named tuples*, which are like records in some other languages:

```
tpl = {name: "Crystal", year: 2017} # NamedTuple(name: String, year: Int32)
tpl[:name]                          # => "Crystal" (String)
```

As tuples are fixed-size and stack-allocated, they're very efficient. Also, the compiler can see the type at each position. This is in contrast to arrays, which can change in size, so you should give preference to tuples over arrays if the size is constant and there are different types.

In the case of symbol or string type keys, you can use the named tuples notation:

```
# Instead of {:key1 => 'a', :key2 => 'b'} you can use:
{key1: 'a', key2: 'b'}
# Instead of {"key1" => 'a', "key2" => 'b'} you can use:
{"key1": 'a', "key2": 'b'}
```

If you don't need names, indexes, or order, but you need to store unique values, use a set:

```
set = Set{41, 42, 43} # => Set{41, 42, 43}
set.class              # => Set(Int32)
# The above is equivalent to
set = Set(Int32).new
set << 42
set << 41
set << 43
set << 41
set                    # => Set{42, 41, 43}
```

Your Turn 4

➤ Destructuring: What are the values of the variables on the left side?

```
var1, var2, var3 = [78, 56, 42]  # array
var1, var2, var3 = {78, 56, 42}  # tuple
```

This is a nice way to get values out of an array or a tuple. We can use it in our currency convertor to replace:

```
arr = input.split(" - ")
curr = arr[0]
rate = arr[1]
```

with:

```
curr, rate = input.split(" - ")
```

From the preceding examples, it's clear that Array, Tuple, Hash, and Set can take different types for their items, while their methods work for all these types. You could say that they have a Type T or K or V as a parameter, like Array(T), Hash(K, V), and so on, where T is Int32 or String or Char or whatever type. In other words: they're *generic types*. In Chapter 6, you'll see how to define your own generic classes that are able to work on any type.

Nilable Types

How do you declare a variable that's of a certain type but can also be nil, sometimes called *nilable*? You saw earlier that in certain situations, Crystal will assign a union type to an object at compile time. You could declare a nilable type as a union type, but you can also declare its type with a ? appended, as shown here:

```
types_and_control_flow/type_nil.cr
n : Int32 | Nil
n = 42
p typeof(n) # => Int32

a : Int32?
a = 42
p typeof(a) # => Int32

b : Int32?
b = nil
p typeof(b) # => Nil

a.try { p a + 1 } # => 43
b.try { p b + 1 } # => no error!
```

When using nilable types, the try method can come in handy: the compiler won't signal any errors when the value might be nil. But be aware that if you lock out the compiler here, you're on your own!

Now it's time to work with union types yourself:

Your Turn 5

➤ a. Union types

In the following code snippet, what's the type of mineral? Write an if statement to show the value of mineral in all cases:

```
arr = ["anadite", "humite", "roselite"]
mineral = arr[4]?
```

➤ b. Here are two empty hashes constructed with union types. What are the key and value types? Add key-value pairs to them so that all types are used, and also add a pair that doesn't compile.

```
h1 = Hash(Int32 | Char, Int32).new
h2 = {} of String | Int32 => Bool | String
```

➤ c. What is the compile-time type and the runtime type of var1 after the following if statements, and why is this?

```
if rand < 0.5
  var1 = 7
end # branches that are not present return nil!
#
var1 = 42
if rand < 0.5
  var1 = "Crystal"
end
#
var1 = 42
if rand < 0.7
  var1 = "Crystal"
else
  var1 = true
end
#
if rand < 0.5
  var1 = 42
else
  var1 = "Crystal"
end
var2 = var1 * 2
var3 = var1 - 1 # <= What does this return ?
```

Controlling the Flow and Types

So far, types have mostly been about keeping our programs out of trouble. While that safety is useful, Crystal also offers many approaches so you can write code whose flow is determined by the types of data it's processing. This simplifies the challenge of keeping code concise while accepting many different kinds of information.

Controlling the Flow, on page 28 showed you how to work with flow constructs, and you saw that a variable is never nil or false in the if-branch. Also, if you have an if var1 && var2, both var1 and var2 are guaranteed not to be nil. Those basics are useful, but Crystal offers many more possibilities.

Instead of using explicit ifs, you can use a more compact ternary form, as shown here:

```
var1 = if 1 > 2  3  else 4 end # => 4
# stated more concisely
var2 = 1 > 2 ? 3 : 4 #=> 4
```

What is the compile-time type of var1 in?

```
# random choice between number and string
var1 = rand < 0.5 ? 42 : "Crystal" #=> 42 or "Crystal"
```

You guessed it: the union type Int32 | String. This means that calling the abs method on var1 won't work:

```
typeof(var1) # => (Int32 | String)
var1.abs # => Error: undefined method 'abs' for String
```

If you could be certain that var1 is an Int32, you could also make the compiler believe that by using as to restrict the type:

```
ivar1 = var1.as(Int32)
```

In this particular case, you can't be certain because of rand, and if var1 turns out to be of type String, the as casting would give a runtime error:

```
cast from String to Int32 failed (TypeCastError)
```

To prevent that, use the as? variant, which returns nil instead of an exception, so you can test it in an if:

```
ivar1 = var1.as?(Int32) # => 42 or nil
# or retaining only the value 42 with if:
if ivar1 = var1.as?(Int32)
  p ivar1.abs # => 42
end
```

Explicitly testing that var1 is nil can be done with the following:

```
if var1.nil?
  # here var1 is nil
end
```

But this should almost never be necessary. Simply use if var1 with the else branch to handle the nil case.

You can test the type of an object with the is_a? method. Inside such an if, the object is guaranteed to be of that type:

```
var1 = 42
if var1.is_a?(Number)
  # here var1 is a Number, which can be integer or floating point
end
```

If you have to test on a number of types, it's better to use case:

```
case var1
when Number
  p var1 + 42
when String
  p "we have a string"
else
  p "var1 is not a number or a string"
end
# => 84
```

case is a very versatile construct: it can use all kinds of variables, including symbols, enums, and tuples. Not only can it test on the type of the variable, but it can also invoke a method on it, as in this snippet:

```
num = 42
case num
when .even?
  puts "you have an even number"
when .odd?
  puts "you have an odd number"
end
# => you have an even number
```

Using a tuple variable together with case makes some pattern matching possible. FizzBuzz is a common programming question in which you're asked to print out "FizzBuzz" if a number is divisible by 3 and 5, "Fizz" if divisible by 3, and "Buzz" if divisible by 5, counting from 1 to 100. case enables you to write a compact version:

```
(1..100).each do |i|
  case {i % 3, i % 5}
  when {0, 0}
    puts "FizzBuzz"
  when {0, _}
    puts "Fizz"
  when {_, 0}
    puts "Buzz"
  else
    puts i
  end
end
```

% is the modulo operation, which returns the remainder from integer division. Note that you can use one (or more) _ when testing a tuple if that value doesn't matter.

Another way to deal with types is to see if the contents of a variable can reply to a given method call. Safely testing that is done with responds_to?:

```
var1 = "Crystal"
if var1.responds_to?(:abs)  # false in this case
  var1.abs
end
```

Your Turn 6

➤ a. What is the value of var1 after this if?

```
if var1 = 1
    puts "inside if"
    var1 = 2
    puts var1
end
```

This behavior is different from many other programming languages!

➤ b. What is the output of the following program?

```
if (num = 9) < 0
  puts "#{num}, is negative"
elsif num < 10
  puts "#{num}, has 1 digit"
else
  puts "#{num}, has multiple digits"
end
```

➤ c. Test this code snippet and explain its behavior. Do you see a way to improve this?

```
begin
  a = 4 + 6
rescue
  puts "an ex occurred"
ensure
  puts a + 42
end
```

Hint: The compiler takes the possibility of an exception into account.

A Company's Story Crystallized: Linkfeed

Kostya Makarchev is the CTO of Linkfeed, a Russian company that focuses on search engine optimization (SEO).

Ivo: *What production projects do you use Crystal for?*

Kostya Makarchev: *In our company, I rewrote a backend API from Ruby (event-machine) to Crystal (21 shards, 300KB source size, compiled size 21MB). This backend has a high load throughput, using Redis and the network. The Ruby version had many concurrency and stability problems (crashed from time to time, slow, had bugs that were hard to debug, nil exceptions). Also, it used a lot of network communications, which we handled with threads or by event-machine, which in Ruby is quite bad.*

The Crystal version has now been in production for over a year, and it is much more stable and faster than the Ruby app: it works without any problems. It comprises an HTTP server, Redis, network connections, HTTP fetching, and an HTML parsing application, all with many concurrency aspects, and running as some 20 background processes.

Ivo: *Why did you decide to use Crystal for these applications?*

Kostya Makarchev: *I like to code in Ruby because I can do it very fast and it is very enjoyable. When I saw Crystal the first time in 2013, I already knew that it should solve all my problems. So first I rewrote a small daemon (200 lines of code) to Crystal in one day, and it just works, executing ten times faster than in Ruby. Later, I rewrote some small projects, and finally I rewrote the big backend project, 300K lines, and rewriting also was quite fast: sometimes I copied part of the Ruby code and it just compiled. I also tried Erlang, Go, and Node.js, but all these languages are not intuitive to code in for me.*

But in Crystal I was amazed that I can code as fast as in Ruby. I can think an idea in my head and then just write code for it, without any pauses for language syntax or how to implement this or that. I just prototype and code my ideas, as fast as I can think. This is a great plus for Ruby or Crystal compared to other languages.

I think Crystal and Go are nice for network applications, or to replace event-machine from Ruby or Node.js projects. Go has better concurrency than Crystal, but Go is hard to think in, or to do fast prototyping, so I don't like it. Also Erlang is nice for network apps, but to code in it is even harder. After using Crystal channel concurrency, I don't like event-machine and Node.js concurrency anymore because they work with callbacks, which are a pain to debug.

Ivo: *What kinds of problems does Crystal solve best?*

Kostya Makarchev: *Background processes, involving HTTP and concurrency.*

Ivo: *What was it like to develop with Crystal?*

Kostya Makarchev: *Rewriting was quite fun because I copied most of the Ruby code, and it worked almost without changes.*

Ivo: *Are there any aspects of Crystal that specifically benefit customer satisfaction?*

Kostya Makarchev: *Of course the speed of the production app, but also that it is rock stable and that it can be installed as one executable.*

Ivo: *What advantages or disadvantages have you experienced from deploying a Crystal application in production?*

Kostya Makarchev: *Deploying is super easy—I just use Capistrano: it compiles the binary on the target server after deploy.*

Ivo: *What do you like the most about Crystal compared to other languages?*

Kostya Makarchev: *I love Crystal as compared to Ruby in network applications because of the type checking, fast execution, and nice concurrency. All this in Ruby is just bad. But right now, I am not going to rewrite Rails apps to Crystal, or apps with a big usage of ActiveRecord because this functionality is not yet completely present in Crystal.*

Wrapping Up

In this chapter, we probed deeper into some basic types and coding techniques, such as symbols, tuples, and the case statement. For a Rubyist, perhaps this isn't all new stuff, but you became more familiar with the Crystal compiler and how it uses union types to make your code more safe. Union types form the cornerstone of Crystal's type system. Armed with this insight, let's start exploring methods and procs and see how Crystal makes good use of overloading in our next chapter.

## CHAPTER 4

Organizing Code in Methods and Procs

While you can write working code line by line without structuring it, you won't usually get very far before you want to be able to reuse code and store logic in more sophisticated ways. Methods (sometimes called functions) let you group code into chunks, and you give them names so you can call them. In this chapter, you'll see Crystal's approach to methods. It's very Ruby-like, though Crystal's use of types creates some differences on the way to performant and readable code. If you feel the need, review *Using Methods*, on page 33 to get an introduction to methods.

Because everything is an object in Crystal, there are methods on everything, even simple values such as Int32 and Char. Operators such as / or <= are also methods. Everything we'll talk about in this chapter also applies to the methods you'll use in classes (see Chapter 5, *Using Classes and Structs*, on page 89).

Luckily, much of what you know about methods in other languages applies here—we'll review basics in this chapter, but it's worth noting some things up front that may surprise you if you're coming from other languages.

Methods in Crystal don't have to live in a class, in contrast to Java or C#, for example. You can also define them (as we've seen many times in earlier chapters) at the top level of your program. It's also common to group related methods in a module (see *Using Modules as Namespaces*, on page 120) to be included in classes.

Crystal also has a strong sense of scope. Unlike Ruby or Python, Crystal doesn't have global variables at all. Variables that you define locally inside a method won't be visible outside that method. The inverse is also true in Crystal: variables that you define outside of a method won't be visible inside that method, either.

```
methods_and_procs/methods.cr
x = 1

def add(y)
  x + y # Error: undefined local variable or method 'x'
end

add(2)
```

Passing Arguments

Occasionally, you'll create methods you call without passing any information, but usually you want methods to do something specific to your needs. When you call a method, you can supply one or several arguments that give the method information to process. When you use arguments in a method's definition, you have to enumerate them inside parentheses, like the add method in the following example:

```
methods_and_procs/methods.cr
def add(x, y)
  # return x + y   # return is optional
  x + y
end
```

① `add(2, 3)`   `# => 5`
② `add 2, 3`   `# => 5`
③ `add(1.0, 3.14)`   `# => 4.14`
④ `add("Hello ", "Crystal")` `# => "Hello Crystal"`
⑤ `add(42, " times")` `# => Error: no overload matches 'Int32#+' with type String`
⑥ `add`   `# => Error: wrong number of arguments for 'add'`
`# (given 0, expected 2)`

(You might recognize this from *More Safety Through Types*, on page 12.)

When you're calling a method, you can omit the ( ) if you prefer, as in line ❷. This is nice when you have only a few arguments, but it quickly becomes less readable in more complex situations. This book uses both ways as appropriate.

From lines ❶, ❸, and ❹, you see that we can happily use *duck typing*, as in any dynamic language. In duck typing, you let the language figure out the type of an object based on its content. You can use the add method for all objects x and y whose Type has a + method, which is the case here for numbers and strings.

As you'll see shortly, you can specify types, but Crystal vows never to make typing arguments mandatory, unlike most statically typed languages. Duck typing is flexible and makes your code more widely applicable. But sometimes the given parameters aren't suitable, as in line ❺. Then, Crystal relentlessly cuts execution short through a compiler error. Also, as in line ❻, when you give no or not enough arguments, another compiler error is issued: wrong number of arguments for 'add' (given 0, expected 2).

In *More Safety Through Types*, on page 12 in the overloading.cr scripts, which also used the add method, we found out that Crystal allows typing of the arguments. (It might be a good idea to play with it again before continuing.)

Pitfall

In the following snippet, only the y argument is declared to be of type Int, not x:

```
def add(x, y : Int)
  x + y
end

add 3, 4     # 7
add 2.14, 7  # 9.14
```

In the second add call, x isn't of type Int. If x and y should both be of type Int, define the method as: add(x : Int, y : Int).

Crystal offers some more intricate options for working with arguments. You can specify *default* values for arguments at the end of the parameter list, in case a parameter for that argument isn't given, as in this show method:

methods_and_procs/methods.cr
```
def show(x, y = 1, z = 2, w = 3)
  "x: #{x}, y: #{y}, z: #{z}, w: #{w}"
end

show 10          # => "x: 10, y: 1, z: 2, w: 3"
show 10, 10      # => "x: 10, y: 10, z: 2, w: 3"
show 10, 30, 2, 3 # => "x: 10, y: 30, z: 2, w: 3"
show 10, 20      # => "x: 10, y: 20, z: 2, w: 3"

show 10, z: 10            # => "x: 10, y: 1, z: 10, w: 3"
show 10, w: 30, y: 2, z: 3 # => "x: 10, y: 2, z: 3, w: 30"
show y: 10, x: 20        # => "x: 20, y: 10, z: 2, w: 3"
show y: 10               # Error, missing argument: x
```

As you can see in the second series of show calls in the code above, you can specify arguments by name when the method is called. Using *named arguments* implies we aren't tied to their order. Code is also much more readable if we use descriptive names, as in the following example where we construct an authorization client that needs values for the host, client_id, and client_secret arguments:

```
require "oauth2"

client = OAuth2::Client.new(
  host: "martian1",
  client_id: "7594",
  client_secret: "W*GDFUY75HSVS#@!"
)
```

Returning Values

A method returns the value of its last expression, so there's no need to explicitly return that or declare its type. However, if you want to document or directly control that return type, you can explicitly specify the type, as in this example:

methods_and_procs/methods.cr
```
def typed_method : Array(Int32)
  (42..47).to_a.select { |n| n % 4 == 0 }
end

typed_method # => [44]
```

You can also explicitly use Nil as your return type if you want to indicate that this is a so-called side-effect method: only important for what it does, not for what it returns. Developers consuming your method will need to be prepared for that, but at least it shouldn't be a surprise nil.

If you need to return multiple values, you can pack them together in a tuple or an array. Unpack the values by using destructuring (see Unpack the values by using *Your Turn 4*, on page 62):

methods_and_procs/methods.cr
```
# Multiple return values
def triple_and_array(s)
  {s * 3, s.split}
end

# unpacking:
ret = triple_and_array("42")  # => {"424242", ["42"]}
ret[0]                        # => "424242"
ret[1]                        # => ["42"]
# or:
num, arr = triple_and_array("gold")
num # => "goldgoldgold"
arr # => ["gold"]
```

Using the Splat Argument *

If you want your method to accept a variable number of parameters, then you can't give a name to each of your arguments. Instead, use one argument prefixed with a *, to create a so-called *splat* argument. The method can then take from 0 to an unlimited number of parameters because they're all converted into one tuple.

Say, for example, you want to calculate the salaries for an unknown number of employees:

```
methods_and_procs/methods.cr
def salaries(*employees)
  employees.each do |emp|
    # calculate salary
    puts "#{emp}'s salary is: 2500"
  end
end

salaries()           # =>
salaries("Jones") # => Jones's salary is: 2500
salaries("Baudelaire", "Rogers", "Gandhi")

# =>
# Baudelaire's salary is: 2500
# Rogers's salary is: 2500
# Gandhi's salary is: 2500
```

Using the splat argument doesn't mean you have to sort out all of the arguments yourself. Crystal offers a different approach, using just a bare * to indicate that all arguments after the * must be named with labels. That approach works like this:

```
def display(n, *, height, width)
  "The shape has height #{height} and width #{width}"
end

display 3, height: 2, width: 5
# =>  "The shape has height 2 and width 5"
```

You can even give a named parameter another name to use in the method's body so that your code reads more naturally:

```
methods_and_procs/methods.cr
def increment(number, by value)
  number + value
end

p increment(10, by: 10) # => 20
```

Another classic situation is the pesky problem of creating a string of values delimited by a certain character—but that character can't appear after the last value. For example, we want "1-2-3" but not "1-2-3-". This solution takes a variable number of values args, denoting the delimiter as with joiner—joiner is the internal name used inside the method, and with is the name used when calling the method to pass the parameter's value:

```
methods_and_procs/methods.cr
def join(*args, with joiner)
  String.build do |str|
    args.each_with_index do |arg, index|
      str << joiner if index > 0
      str << arg
    end
  end
end

join 1, 2, 3, with: "-"      # => "1-2-3"
join 1, 2, 3, 4, 5, with: "*" # => "1*2*3*4*5"
```

Your Turn 1

➤ a. Total: Write a method total to calculate the sum of an arbitrary amount of numbers. Change total so that the sum starts from an initial value.

➤ b. Splat a Tuple:

You can also unpack a tuple (which we explored in *Your Turn 4*, on page 62) directly into the arguments of a method. Suppose you want to do this:

```
def add(n, m)
  n + m
end

tpl = {42, 108}
add tpl
```

Does this work? Can you explain this?

You have to call it like this: add *tpl, which is called *splatting a tuple*. If tpl is a named tuple and you want to use the argument names, you have to use a double splat **. Try that out.

Another trick[1] uses **argument to capture a variable number of named parameters into a named tuple.

Working with Yield, Procs, and Blocks

While named methods are typically the core of an application, sometimes you want to be able to manipulate your logic more flexibly. Procs let you put logic, including methods, into variable-like structures that you can pass through

---

1. https://crystal-lang.org/docs/syntax_and_semantics/splats_and_tuples.html

your program and call explicitly or through the yield keyword. Like methods, Procs can take arguments and return values.

This is bread and butter for a Rubyist, but if you don't know Ruby, this subject can be a bit confusing at first. For non-Rubyists, *Using Procs*, on page 78 may be an easier if usually more verbose place to start with these concepts.

Blocks let you reuse code without creating formal methods, once you learn how the syntax works. (You've already been using them, but they have many options.) You can group one or more code lines into a block of code by surrounding them with { } or a do end. They aren't methods, but they do have a name for later reference.

As in Ruby, you can also use these code blocks as parameters in a method call—for example, if testing is a method, you could call it with a code block:

```
testing do
  puts "in code block"
end
```

If you create a method that uses that name, yield will call that code block:

```
def testing
  puts "at top of method"
  yield
  puts "back inside method"
  yield
  puts "at end of method"
end
# =>
# at top of method
# in code block
# back inside method
# in code block
# at end of method
```

When you call these blocks with yield, the Crystal compiler always inlines them for performance. They don't cause a jump to a separate function during execution. You can use blocks for readability or reusing code, and it won't negatively affect performance. This mechanism can come in handy, for instance, if you want to iterate over a collection or provide a custom algorithm.

yield behaves like a method call, so you can give it one or more parameters by adding them to the do block as do |n|, as in this version:

methods_and_procs/procs.cr

```
def testing
  puts "at top of method"
  yield 1
  puts "back inside method"
  yield 2
  puts "at end of method"
end

testing do |n|
  puts "in code block #{n}"
end

# =>
# at top of method
# in code block 1
# back inside method
# in code block 2
# at end of method
```

You can use break inside a block to exit early from the method—next exits early from the block, but not from the method.

Is a code block also an object? Technically, no. But you can *capture* the block when you're writing it like def testing(&block). This will create a Proc object for the block (which you defined with testing do ...) that's passed in. That allows you to treat it as a normal object and include it in arguments or return values. But you have to use the Proc method call instead of yield. In this case, you must use block.call.

methods_and_procs/procs.cr

```
def testing(&block)
  puts "at top of method"
  block.call
  puts "back inside method"
  block.call
  puts "at end of method"
end

testing do
  puts "in code block"
end
# =>
# at top of method
# in code block
# back inside method
# in code block
# at end of method
```

If the code you want to execute in your block is brief, you may instead want to use a code block defined with { }. This puts the code block logic near the call and makes it easy to write concise yet readable code for repeated logic.

```
methods_and_procs/procs.cr
langs = %w[Java Go Crystal]
langs.map { |lang| lang.upcase } # => ["JAVA", "GO", "CRYSTAL"]
```

That block has only one argument with a single method call on it. In that case, Crystal lets you apply some nice syntax sugar (that's different from Ruby). In the following example, the map method is applied to each string in langs, uppercasing it. Both lines produce the same result. You'll see that the block and variable syntax is replaced by &.

```
methods_and_procs/procs.cr
langs = %w[Java Go Crystal]
langs.map { |lang| lang.upcase } # => ["JAVA", "GO", "CRYSTAL"]
langs.map &.upcase               # => ["JAVA", "GO", "CRYSTAL"]
```

The method can be an operator as well, and it can also take arguments, as it does here:

```
methods_and_procs/procs.cr
nums = [42, 43, 44]
nums.map { |num| num + 2 } # (1) => [44, 45, 46]
nums.map &.+(2)            # (2) => [44, 45, 46]
```

You can also chain methods (see *Chaining Methods*, on page 52) with this.

Putting It Together—Converting Currencies 3

Let's see how we could output some monetary conversions using a code block:

```
methods_and_procs/curr_conv5.cr
base = "USD"
rates = {
  "EUR" => 0.84320536,
  "CAD" => 1.26761115,
  "CNY" => 6.61591576,
}
full_names = {
  "EUR" => "Euro",
  "CAD" => "Canadian Dollar",
  "CNY" => "Chinese Yuan",
}

# How much is 1 US Dollar?
output = "1 #{base} = \n" +  # (1)
         rates.keys.map do |curr|  # (2)
           "\t#{rates[curr]} #{full_names[curr]}s (#{curr})"
         end.join("\n")  # (3)
```

```
puts output
# 1 USD =
#      0.84320536 Euros (EUR)
#      1.26761115 Canadian Dollars (CAD)
#      6.61591576 Chinese Yuans (CNY)

puts
# How much is 42 US Dollars?
amount = 42
output = "#{amount} #{base} = \n" +
         rates.keys.map do |curr|
           temp = sprintf("%3.2f", amount * rates[curr]) # (4)
           "\t#{temp} #{full_names[curr]}s (#{curr})"
         end.join("\n")
puts output
# 42 USD =
#      35.41 Euros (EUR)
#      53.24 Canadian Dollars (CAD)
#      277.87 Chinese Yuans (CNY)
```

(1) Start with a string called output.

(2) Add to this string the result of a code block. This iterates over an array with all the currencies given by rates.keys. For each currency map accepts a code block that makes an output string. map produces a new array with output strings for the original currency array.

(3) Join all items of this array into a string, with newlines between items separated by a newline.

(4) Round off the output to two decimal numbers, using sprintf and a format string, "%3.2f".

Your Turn 2

➤ Syntax Sugar

- Compute the third power (hint: use **) of the numbers from 1 to 10.

- Sort the langs array from the previous example by the size of the strings (hint: use the sort_by method).

- Reverse sort all letters from the languages in langs. The result must be: ["vaaJ", "oG", "ytsrlaC"]. (Hint: Use chaining.)

Using Procs

In the previous section, you saw that a captured code block (remember the &block) is, in fact, an object, called a Proc or a *lambda* or *anonymous function*;

you can think of a Proc as a function object with a call method. You can create them using a few different approaches:

1) The -> notation lets you create a Proc literal. Here you'll write your add method for two numbers as a Proc:

```
methods_and_procs/procs.cr
fn = ->(n : Int32, m : Int32) { n + m }
typeof(fn)      # => Proc(Int32, Int32, Int32)
fn.call(42, 108) # => 150
```

The Proc's name is on the lefthand side of = . Then the -> is followed by the parameter list. Note that you must use types here. The code body then follows between { } braces. The compiler will infer the return type of a Proc.

2) You can create a Proc from an existing add method using a similar notation:

```
methods_and_procs/procs.cr
def add(n, m)
  n + m
end

fn = ->add(Int32, Int32)
fn.call(42, 108) # => 150
```

3) Because Proc is a class in the standard library, it allows you to also use the new method:

```
methods_and_procs/procs.cr
fn = Proc(Int32, Int32, Int32).new { |n, m| n + m }
fn.call(42, 108) # => 150
```

As in many other languages, Procs can work as *closures*, which means they can capture connections to variables used at the time the Proc was created. This works for Proc literals:

```
methods_and_procs/procs.cr
n = 42
fn = ->(m : Int32) { n + m }
fn.call(108) # => 150
n = 20
fn.call(108) # => 128
```

As you can see, the value of n is known in the Proc, and it also knows when n changes its value.

Captured blocks have the same behavior with variables:

```
methods_and_procs/procs.cr
def capture(&block : Int32 -> Int32)
  block
end

n = 42
proc = capture { |m| n + m }
proc.call(108) # => 150
n = 20
proc.call(108) # => 128
```

This also shows that a captured block can have a type annotation: Int32 -> Int32 means: take an Int32 as parameter, and return an Int32. To take two Int32 parameters, you'd write: Int32, Int32 -> Int32.

Your Turn 3

➤ ReturnProc: Write an increment method (incr) that initializes a counter to 0 and returns the increment through a Proc. Print out its type and call it a few times. What happens when you give the method a new name and call it with that name a few times?

Is your head spinning right now? The possible syntax combinations of code-blocks and procs can sometimes be overused. But there are clever uses, such as storing a Proc in an instance variable to simulate an event-handler (see *Defining Callbacks*, on page 112).

Treat yourself to a cup of coffee or a good movie!

Overloading and Multiple Dispatch

Crystal allows you to have different versions of a method with the same name. This is called *overloading*. *More Safety Through Types*, on page 12 showed how you can use argument types to restrict methods.

Code written without types can be more generic and reusable, but specifying types can often make code safer. Details such as the number of arguments, their names, and whether the method accepts a code block let you craft different versions of a method that work with slightly different contexts or arguments.

The compiler creates separate executable code for each version of a method. Then, when the compiler encounters calls to that method name, the compiler attaches the right code version, based on the best-matching type of the parameter(s). You can have code specialization based on type without needing any checks at runtime, which adds considerably to execution speed.

To see this for yourself, try out the following. Copy all the add methods and the tests from overloading1234.cr (see *More Safety Through Types*, on page 12). Then write and test an add method that takes:

- A number and a Boolean, returning the number if the Boolean is true, otherwise returning 0.

- Two strings, converts them to integers and then adds them.

What happens if you execute the previous tests? Use what you learned in *Getting Input*, on page 46 to handle this.

There's still a challenge to sort out. After defining a method, add(x : String, y : String), the test case, add("Hello ", "Crystal"), will now take this new method for execution instead of the generic add. The reason is that the types in this call better match the new method. But now to_i will fail on these arguments, giving rise to an exception.

You can protect your new method against this:

```
def add(x : String, y : String)
  if x.to_i? && y.to_i?
    add x, y # calls version 1
  end
end
```

But add("Hello ", "Crystal") will then return nil, so you need an else branch for that:

```
def add(x : String, y : String)
  if x.to_i? && y.to_i?
    add x, y # calls version 1
  else
    x + y
  end
end
```

Here's the complete code of this example:

methods_and_procs/overloading.cr
```
# version 1:
def add(x : Int, y : Int)
  x + y
end

# version 2:
def add(x : Number, y : Number)
  x + y
end
```

```
# version 3:
def add(x : Number, y : String)
  x.to_s + y # convert a number to a string with to_s method
end

# version 4:
def add(x, y)
  x + y
end

# new methods:
# version 5:
def add(x : Number, y : Bool)
  y ? x : 0
end

# version 6:
def add(x : String, y : String)
  if x.to_i? && y.to_i?
    add x.to_i, y.to_i # calls version 1
  else
    x + y
  end
end

add(2, 3)                 # => 5
add(1.0, 3.14)            # => 4.14
add("Hello ", "Crystal")  # => "Hello Crystal"
add(42, " times")         # => "42 times"
add 5, true               # => 5
add 13, false             # => 0
add("12", "13")           # => 25
```

You can also make this work with a union type on the return value. In a new script, make an add(x, y) method that returns nil if y is equal to 0, and x + y otherwise. Test with n = add(2, 3). What is n's type? What happens when you try to execute n + 10? Add an if test that prevents this.

When the arguments have union types, the compiler doesn't know which method version to call. Only at runtime is the real type of the arguments known and the right method version called accordingly. This is called *multiple dispatch*. But this doesn't hamper speed too much because versions for all the possible types were compiled ahead of time. You can see this here:

methods_and_procs/overloading3.cr
```
def display(x : Number) # overloading 1
  puts "#{x} is a number"
end

def display(x : String) # overloading 2
  puts "#{x} is a string"
end
```

```
n = 42
display n # => 42 is a number

str = "magic"
display str # => magic is a string

r = rand < 0.5 ? n : str
typeof(r) # => (Int32 | String)
display r
```

In the first display, call overloading 1 is used. In the second, overloading 2, both decided at compile time.

But the situation is different for the third call: the compile-time type of r is (Int32 | String). Which of these types r will become is only known at runtime because of rand, so which display method to call can only be decided then!

You can also use type restrictions for a splat argument, as you can see here:

methods_and_procs/overloading3.cr
```
def method1(*args : Int32)
end

def method1(*args : String)
end

method1 41, 42, 43              # OK, invokes first overload
method1 "Crystal", "Ruby", "Go" # OK, invokes second overload
method1 1, 2, "No"
# Error: no overload matches 'method1' with types Int32, Int32, String
method1() # Error: no overload matches 'method1'
```

Note that the last two calls of method1 are rejected by the compiler.

Using a Shorter Syntax for Exception Handling

Remember how we got input from the user to fill in an array and handled a possible exception with begin/rescue in *Getting Input*, on page 46? You can write that kind of code much more succinctly. First, let's rewrite that code with a few methods to give it more structure:

methods_and_procs/exceptions.cr
```
puts "Enter the numbers one by one, and end with an empty line:"
input_array # => for example: [78, 56, 12]

def input_array
  arr = [] of Int8
  while number = gets
    number = number.strip # removes leading or trailing whitespace
    if number == "" || number == "stop"
      break
    end
```

```
    add_to_array(arr, number)
  end
  arr
end

def add_to_array(arr, number)
  begin
    arr << number.to_i8
  rescue
    puts "integer bigger than 255"
  end
end
```

The method add_to_array now handles the possible exception. You can write this more concisely by leaving out the begin keyword, as shown here:

methods_and_procs/exceptions2.cr
```
def add_to_array(arr, number)
  arr << number.to_i8
rescue
  puts "integer bigger than 255"
end
```

This shorthand also works for ensure, which is usually used for freeing resources or cleaning up.

Using Recursive Methods

A method can call itself—for example, here you'll calculate the factorial of an integer in a method, fact:

methods_and_procs/factorial.cr
```
def fact(n)
  n == 0 ? 1 : n * fact(n - 1)
end

fact(5) # => 120
```

This method happily accepts any argument, but look what happens when you feed it a negative integer or a string:

```
fact(-2) # => Runtime error: Invalid memory access
(signal 11) at address 0x7ffbff7fdff8
fact("Crystal") # => Error: undefined method '-' for String
```

You can make your code more robust by using types and handling exceptions:

```
methods_and_procs/factorial2.cr
def fact(n : Int) : Int
  if n < 0
    raise ("n cannot be negative!")
  end
  n == 0 ? 1 : n * fact(n - 1)
end

fact(5) # => 120

begin
  fact(-2) # => Runtime error: n cannot be negative! (Exception)
rescue ex
  p ex.message
end
# => "n cannot be negative!"

fact("Crystal") # => Error: no overload matches 'fact' with type String
```

Now your program doesn't crash: the raised exception is caught, and its message is displayed. And giving a string argument is stopped at compilation with a clear message about wrong argument types.

But if you don't want to use the heavy begin-rescue clause, simply print out the error message and exit the program:

```
methods_and_procs/factorial3.cr
def fact(n : Int) : Int
  if n < 0
    puts "n must be positive!"
    exit
  end
  n == 0 ? 1 : n * fact(n - 1)
end

fact(5)  # => 120
fact(-2) # => "n must be positive!"
```

It's a good idea to test defensively when entering any method, especially recursive ones. This approach also lets you exit from deep recursion easily. Return immediately from the method when a necessary condition isn't met. For example:

```
def some_method(n : Int)
  return nil unless n > 1
  # other code, here n is > 1
end
```

You could return nil or false or any other value that you see fit. Some people like to use unless here because it states the condition that has to be fulfilled, so it may be easier to understand. Remember that errors are expensive. Raise errors only when a condition needs special attention.

Tail Calls Add Up

Some languages derived from Ruby, notably Elixir, are designed to let recursion go infinitely deep as long as the function doesn't require tracking additional information. When possible, they perform what is called tail call optimization, explicitly looking for recursive function calls in the last line of a function, and removing the normal overhead that would track the calls.

Crystal doesn't explicitly support tail call optimization, though the LLVM compiler underneath sometimes does that work. While you can make recursion go a long way, you may find limits to how deep you can go in a variety of circumstances.

Your Turn 4

➤ BubbleSort: Implement the Bubblesort[2] algorithm for sorting an array, using the pseudocode you'll find there. Make a copy of the input using the dup method. Write two versions of the algorithm, as an ascending and descending sort, using yield and a code block for each version.

A Company's Story Crystallized: Duo Design

Cris Ward is Company Director at Duo Web Design,[3] which is a web design agency focusing on delivering dynamic web and digital solutions. It is based in Manchester, U.K.

> **Ivo:** *What production projects do you use Crystal for?*
>
> **Cris Ward:** *Our main project is Duo CMS (Content Management System); it is in it's fifth incarnation as Duo CMS 5. In active development since 2004, the server part of the system has undergone a recent rewrite in Crystal to make it more flexible and performant for the modern web. We utilise our CMS system for most of our customer websites and web applications as it provides us a high level of customization to achieve the best balance between performance and ease of use for our clients.*
>
> **Ivo:** *Why did you decide to use Crystal for these applications?*

---

2.   https://en.wikipedia.org/wiki/Bubble_sort

3.   https://www.duodesign.co.uk/

Cris Ward: At Duo, we've been using Node.js as our server platform of choice for a number of years. Node is designed to do every task asynchronously. This means that, by default, if you ask it to do five tasks, it will try and do all of them at the same time. Node solves this with promises, allowing the programmer to chain together a series of asynchronous tasks into a series of individual steps performed one after another.

On the server, having parallel tasks as the default seems like a very efficient idea. In reality, most of the tasks we perform as developers require data from the previous task. Even when we can perform the tasks in parallel, the resources of the system can get quickly exhausted—i.e., making lots of parallel requests to the database can exhaust your pool of connections and lower the number of concurrent users you can serve.

During our years using node, creating promise chains became normal. Half the code written was about turning async tasks into sequential tasks. These chains became difficult to test, debug, and understand. It can be very difficult, just by looking at the code, to see in which order the tasks, and various sub-tasks, are executed.

Ivo: What kinds of problems does Crystal solve best?

Cris Ward: We use it with great success as a server-side processing language, running SQL queries against a database, utilizing ORMs, reading and writing files, and linking with third-party APIs.

Ivo: What was it like to develop with Crystal?

Cris Ward: This is what I found when rewriting our server-side CMS:

• Crystal is quick, in my tests often x2 as quick as Node for my use case.

• It uses very little memory—typically greater than 5MB versus less than 200MB per process for Node.

• It has an excellent standard library, so we have only 12 dependencies in total, compared to Node's 100s.

• Code looks synchronous by default. It uses an event loop like node, but Fibers, which communicate through channels like Go, are used for concurrency. This makes code much easier to follow.

• Crystal is statically typed so it tells you at compile time if you've made any errors.

• Crystal's type system infers types so it's very easy to use as you don't need to use type annotations very often.

Ivo: Are there any aspects of Crystal that specifically benefit customer satisfaction?

Cris Ward: Its execution speed, and the early detection of possible errors during development, saving us and our customers some headaches.

Ivo: What advantages or disadvantages have you experienced from deploying a Crystal application in production?

Cris Ward: *The DuoCMS 5 server code written in Node.js is around 15,609 lines of JavaScript; DuoCMS 6, rewritten in Crystal, is about 10,186 lines. At this point in time, DuoCMS 6 actually has more features with 30 percent fewer lines of code and no confusing control flow! Compare some of the Node and Crystal code here: https://www.duodesign.co.uk/blog/from-node-to-crystal/.*

Ivo: *What do you like the most about Crystal, compared to other languages?*

Cris Ward: *While using Node, I evaluated lots of other languages and platforms, including Python, PHP, Ruby, and Go. They tended to be either slower than node or not as nice to write. Speed and syntax are both things within a language that you can optimise but never really improve beyond a certain point. When I read about Crystal, I decided to emulate some of the server-side portions of our content management system. This turned out to be pretty awesome. I enjoyed writing Crystal so much that we've recreated our whole CMS backend in Crystal. Also, our website is rewritten in Crystal.*

Wrapping Up

We hope you're convinced by now that Crystal is quite versatile in the way it handles method arguments. It has no trouble accepting and returning many values. Overloading through type restrictions makes your code more robust and often more performant, while using Procs wisely can make it more versatile.

In the next chapter, we'll talk about classes and structs. Let's see what Crystal brings to the table there.

## CHAPTER 5

Using Classes and Structs

If you've done much object-oriented development, you're familiar with classes. You might also have noticed, though, that the details of classes vary from language to language. In this chapter, you'll see Crystal's specific take on classes, and you'll learn the ins and outs of working with classes. You'll learn how to construct a class and a struct, how to use inheritance, and how to control visibility of methods. Along the way, you'll master syntactic details.

In object-oriented code, methods don't stand alone most of the time: they form the action part of a class, and they're the only way to interact with objects. You should only find out the data part of an object (its internal state) by using methods. This is also true in Crystal. But, as we saw earlier, methods can also be used standalone or in modules, providing a more functional approach to coding.

You know that everything in Crystal is an object. Each object has a runtime type, which corresponds to the name of its class and responds to certain methods. You also know that during compilation, things can be a bit more complicated: the compile-time type given by typeof determines which code gets generated and protects you from annoying errors.

When performance is a big concern for your project and simpler value types sound appealing, Crystal also offers structs as a possible alternative to classes.

Converting a Ruby Class to Crystal

If you're a Ruby developer, converting classes is a place where the differences between the languages are especially visible. Walking through the transition from Ruby to Crystal with explanations of the error messages along the way can make it easier to see how Crystal's use of types changes the story. (If you're not a Ruby developer, feel free to skip to the next section.)

Here's a simple class in Ruby:

classes_and_structs/mineral.rb

```ruby
class Mineral
  attr_reader :name, :hardness, :crystal_struct

  def initialize(name, hardness, crystal_struct)
    @name = name
    @hardness = hardness
    @crystal_struct = crystal_struct
  end
end

def mineral_with_crystal_struct(crstruct, minerals)
  minerals.find { |m| m.crystal_struct == crstruct }
end

def longest_name(minerals)
  minerals.map { |m| m.name }.max_by { |name| name.size }
end
```

Now let's add some test data and see if it works:

classes_and_structs/mineral.rb

```ruby
minerals = [
  Mineral.new("gold", 1, 'cubic'),
  Mineral.new("topaz", 8, 'orthorombic'),
  Mineral.new("apatite", 5, 'hexagonal'),
  Mineral.new("wolframite", 4.5, 'monoclinic'),
  Mineral.new("calcite", 3, 'trigonal'),
  Mineral.new("diamond", 10, 'cubic'),
]

min = mineral_with_crystal_struct('hexagonal', minerals)
puts "#{min.crystal_struct} - #{min.name} - #{min.hardness}"
# => hexagonal - apatite - 5

puts longest_name(minerals)
# => wolframite
```

Running this program in a terminal with $ ruby mineral.rb shows the following:

```
apatite - hexagonal - 5
wolframite
```

Everything seems okay, but what if no mineral with the specified crystal structure exists in your array?

```
classes_and_structs/mineral.rb
# Runtime error:
min = mineral_with_crystal_struct('triclinic', minerals)
puts "#{min.crystal_struct} - #{min.name} - #{min.hardness}"
# 3.5_mineral.rb:39:in `<main>': undefined method 'crystal_struct'
# for nil:NilClass (NoMethodError)
```

Ruby throws a runtime error at you because find returns nil when it can't find a match. Forgetting to check for a nil return value isn't always as obvious as it is here.

Crystal would prefer to spare you those problems. While converting this Ruby code to Crystal, you'll run into a lot of errors. Don't worry—it's all for the good, and you'll learn to appreciate Crystal's character!

Let's now look at how Crystal deals with this: Save your Ruby code in mineral.cr and build it with $ crystal mineral.cr.

Crystal syntax isn't quite Ruby syntax, so you'll run into an error immediately:

```
Syntax error in mineral.cr:20: unterminated char literal,
use double quotes for strings

Mineral.new("gold", 1, 'cubic'),
                         ^
```

Ruby allows both single and double quotes for strings, but Crystal does not! You'll need to replace all single-quoted strings with double-quoted ones and then compile again:

An error reports another difference:

```
Error in mineral.cr:2: undefined method 'attr_reader'

attr_reader :name, :hardness, :crystal_struct
^~~~~~~~~~~
```

Crystal uses the getter keyword (in fact, it's a macro, see *DRY Your Code with Macros*, on page 151) instead of attr_reader, setter instead of attr_writer, and property instead of attr_accessor. (There are a few other superficial differences between Ruby and Crystal, but not that many. For an overview, see Appendix 2, *Porting Ruby Code to Crystal*, on page 205.)

You can use the name for the property. It doesn't need to be a symbol. Replacing attr_reader with getter and compiling for the third time yields yet another error, which now points us to an essential difference with Ruby. This message is verbose. Don't worry—we'll only show this once:

```
Error in mineral.cr:20:
instantiating 'Mineral:Class#new(String, Int32, String)'
Mineral.new("gold", 1, "cubic"),
      ^~~

in mineral.cr:5:
Can't infer the type of instance variable '@name' of Mineral

The type of a instance variable, if not declared explicitly with
`@name : Type`, is inferred from assignments to it across
the whole program.

The assignments must look like this:
1. `@name = 1` (or other literals), inferred to the literal's type
2. `@name = Type.new`, type is inferred to be Type
3. `@name = Type.method`, where `method` has a return type
 annotation, type is inferred from it
4. `@name = arg`, with 'arg' being a method argument with a
 type restriction 'Type', type is inferred to be Type
5. `@name = arg`, with 'arg' being a method argument with a
 default value, type is inferred using rules 1, 2 and 3 from it
6. `@name = uninitialized Type`, type is inferred to be Type
7. `@name = LibSome.func`, and `LibSome` is a `lib`, type
 is inferred from that fun.
8. `LibSome.func(out @name)`, and `LibSome` is a `lib`, type
 is inferred from that fun argument.

Other assignments have no effect on its type.
Can't infer the type of instance variable '@name' of Mineral
@name = name
^~~~~
```

Here, Crystal clearly can't figure out the type of the instance variable @name, and it wants us to specify it. We specified @name = name, and that's not enough. You can fix this by declaring the type of @name as follows: getter name : String. You should do it for the other properties as well:

```
getter name : String
getter hardness : Int32
getter crystal_struct : String
```

Yet another compile-time error emerges:

```
Error in mineral.cr:25: instantiating
 'Mineral:Class#new(String, Float64, String)'
Mineral.new("wolframite", 4.5, "monoclinic"),
    ^~~

in mineral.cr:8: instance variable '@hardness' of Mineral
must be Int32, not Float64
@hardness = hardness
^~~~~~~~~~
```

Okay, wolframite has a hardness of 4.5, and this isn't an integer. You can replace the @hardness declaration with: getter hardness : Float64, but then the compiler complains that the hardness for the other minerals is still Int32. Better convert the hardness data to floating point numbers.

Another compile run shows us a new error at the "hexagonal" test-data:

```
Error in mineral.cr:31: undefined method 'crystal_struct'
for Nil (compile-time type is (Mineral | Nil))
puts "#{min.crystal_struct} - #{min.name} - #{min.hardness}"
            ^~~~

Rerun with --error-trace to show a complete error trace.
```

This will remind you of the nil runtime error you got with Ruby. Crystal gives you more in-depth info when you compile with the following:

```
$ crystal mineral.cr --error-trace
```

namely, a so-called Nil trace:

```
Nil trace:
  mineral.cr:30
min = mineral_with_crystal_struct("hexagonal", minerals)
^~~
  mineral.cr:30
min = mineral_with_crystal_struct("hexagonal", minerals)
      ^~~~~~~~~~~~~~~~~~~~~~~~~~~
  mineral.cr:13
def mineral_with_crystal_struct(crstruct, minerals)
    ^~~~~~~~~~~~~~~~~~~~~~~~~~~
  mineral.cr:14
  minerals.find { |m| m.crystal_struct == crstruct }
                       ^~~~
  /opt/crystal/src/enumerable.cr:409
  def find(if_none = nil)
  /opt/crystal/src/enumerable.cr:410
    each do |elem|
    ^
  /opt/crystal/src/enumerable.cr:413
    if_none
    ^~~~~~~
  /opt/crystal/src/enumerable.cr:409
  def find(if_none = nil)
                    ^
```

A Nil trace backtracks through the code, starting from the undefined method indication to where the offending type came up. This occurred in the find method in enumerable.cr:

def find(if_none = **nil**)

This code shows that find returns nil as a default value for the case where nothing is found.

Crystal Is Written in Crystal

 By the way, the Crystal code standard library is entirely implemented in Crystal itself. For example, you can look at how Crystal codes all of the Enumerable methods if you'd like to at https://github.com/crystal-lang/crystal/blob/master/src/enumerable.cr. Go ahead, I'll wait here.

The compiler signals a possible occurrence of a null-reference exception but without running the code. This avoids complaints from customers about creepy errors, at least this kind of error. As discussed earlier in *No to the Billion-Dollar Mistake*, on page 13, this is one of the highlights of Crystal. The error message also says that the compile-time type is Mineral | Nil.

This is a union-type (see *Using Arrays*, on page 23): normally the variable min references a Mineral object, but if you have no mineral of that specific crystal structure in your data collection, min is nil. Crystal checks whether every method called on min is available for all the types in the union type. If not, bingo: an error.

You can fix this in the same way that you would in Ruby:

```
if min
  puts "#{min.crystal_struct} - #{min.name} - #{min.hardness}"
else
  puts "No mineral found with this crystal structure!"
end
```

If this looks strange to you, revisit our discussion on falsy and truthy at *Controlling the Flow*, on page 28. When min is nil, this amounts to false, and the first branch of the if statement isn't executed. So inside the first branch, we know that the type of min is Mineral and not Nil. In the else branch, it's Nil and not Mineral.

At last, everything works and you get the same output as Ruby did:

```
apatite - hexagonal - 5
wolframite
```

Finally, let's introduce a nice shorthand code syntax (borrowed from Coffee-Script). Instead of:

```
def initialize(name, hardness, crystal_struct)
  @name = name
  @hardness = hardness
  @crystal_struct = crystal_struct
end
```

you can write:

```
def initialize(@name, @hardness, @crystal_struct)
end
```

Instance variables get their value directly from creating the object, @name becomes "gold," @hardness gets value 1.0, and so on:

```
Mineral.new("gold", 1.0, "cubic")
```

You could also type the properties in the initialize method instead of in the getter clause, like this:

```
def initialize(@name : String, @hardness : Float64, @crystal_struct : String)
```

That wasn't so bad, was it?

Here's the complete Crystal code for our program:

classes_and_structs/mineral.cr
```
class Mineral
  getter name : String
  getter hardness : Float64
  getter crystal_struct : String

  def initialize(@name, @hardness, @crystal_struct)
  end
end

def mineral_with_crystal_struct(crstruct, minerals)
  minerals.find { |m| m.crystal_struct == crstruct }
end

def longest_name(minerals)
  minerals.map { |m| m.name }.max_by { |name| name.size }
end

minerals = [
  Mineral.new("gold", 1.0, "cubic"),
  Mineral.new("topaz", 8.0, "orthorombic"),
  Mineral.new("apatite", 5.0, "hexagonal"),
  Mineral.new("wolframite", 4.5, "monoclinic"),
  Mineral.new("calcite", 3.0, "trigonal"),
  Mineral.new("diamond", 10.0, "cubic"),
]

min = mineral_with_crystal_struct("hexagonal", minerals)
if min
  puts "#{min.crystal_struct} - #{min.name} - #{min.hardness}"
else
  puts "No mineral found with this crystal structure!"
end
# => hexagonal - apatite - 5
```

```
min = mineral_with_crystal_struct("triclinic", minerals)
if min
  puts "#{min.crystal_struct} - #{min.name} - #{min.hardness}"
else
  puts "No mineral found with this crystal structure!"
end
# => "No mineral found with this crystal structure!"

puts longest_name(minerals)
# => wolframite
```

Crystal guides you firmly and expects a higher level of quality and thoroughness in your code than Ruby does. When you use Ruby, you have to rely more on your test suite's completeness in order to detect and avoid that kind of mistake.

Structuring a Class

In the previous section, and in *Organizing Code in Classes and Modules*, on page 34, you saw a simple Mineral class. Here's the class code by itself without any additional logic:

```
class Mineral
  getter name : String
  getter hardness : Float64
  getter crystal_struct : String

  def initialize(@name, @hardness, @crystal_struct)  # constructor
  end
end
```

This class has three read-only instance variables: name, hardness, and crystal_struct. Giving them a type is imposed by the Crystal compiler. But you can also do this in the initialize method:

classes_and_structs/classes.cr
```
class Mineral
  getter name, hardness, crystal_struct

  def initialize(@name : String,
                 @hardness : Float64,
                 @crystal_struct : String)
  end
end
```

Default values can be assigned like this:

```
def initialize(@name : String = "unknown", ...)
end
```

Some people use symbols like :hardness for the property name, but it isn't required. A property without a type must have a default value. Or you could give it a value in initialize (try it!). You don't need to define variables at the start of the class.

The new method creates a Mineral object:

```
min1 = Mineral.new("gold", 1.0, "cubic")
min1 # => #<Mineral:0x271cf00 @crystal_struct="cubic",
# =>                                          @hardness=1.0, @name="gold">
min1.object_id # => 41012992 == 0x271cf00
typeof(min1) # => Mineral    # compile-time type
min1.class   # => Mineral    # run-time type
Mineral.class # => Class     # all classes have type Class
```

new is a class method that's created automatically for every class. It allocates memory, calls initialize, and then returns the newly created object. An object is created on the heap and it has an object_id: its memory address. When it gets a new name or when it's passed to a method, only the reference is passed. This means the object is changed when it's changed in the method.

When you're not sure which types your initialize method will accept, you can also use generic types like T, as in this class Mineralg:

```
classes_and_structs/classes.cr
class Mineralg(T)
  getter name

  def initialize(@name : T)
  end
end

min = Mineralg.new("gold")
min2 = Mineralg.new(42)
min3 = Mineralg(String).new(42)

# => Error: no overload matches 'Mineralg(String).new' with type Int32
```

When naming instance variables, prefix them with @. For *class variables*, use @@, like the @@planet our mineral species comes from. All objects built using this class will share this variable, and its value will be the same to all of them. (However, subclasses, which you'll see in the next section, all get their own copy with the value shared across the subclass.)

To name properties that can change, such as quantity in the code that follows, prefix them with property. For write-only properties that can't be read, use the prefix setter, like id in the following code. Trying to show them is an error:

```
classes_and_structs/classes.cr
class Mineral
  @@planet = "Earth"

  getter name, hardness, crystal_struct
  setter id
  property quantity : Float32

  def initialize(@id : Int32, @name : String, @hardness : Float64,
                 @crystal_struct : String)
    @quantity = 0f32
  end

  def self.planet
    @@planet
  end
end
min1 = Mineral.new(101, "gold", 1.0, "cubic")
min1.quantity = 453.0f32 # => 453.0
min1.id                  # => Error: undefined method 'id' for Mineral
Mineral.planet           # => "Earth"

min2 = min1.dup
min1 == min2 # => false
```

You must make sure that properties are always initialized, either in the initialize method or when calling new. The names of methods called on the class itself are prefixed with self., like the planet method.

Use the dup method to create a "shallow" copy of the object: the copy min2 is a different object, but if the original contains fields that are objects themselves, these are not copied. If you need a "deep" copy, you have to define a clone method.

You can also optionally write a finalize method for a class, which is automatically invoked when an object is garbage collected:

```
def finalize
  puts "Bye bye from this #{self}!"
end
```

But this creates a burden for the garbage collection process. You should use it only if you want to free resources taken by external libraries that the Crystal garbage collector won't free for you. Add this code snippet to see finalization at work, but be warned: you'll exhaust your machine's memory by digging so much gold. So save anything you need before running it.

```
loop do
  Mineral.new(101, "gold", 1.0, "cubic")
end
```

As in Ruby or C#, you can *reopen a class*, which means making additional definitions of a class: they're all combined into a single class. This even works for built-in classes. How cool is it to define your own new methods on existing classes, such as String or Array? (Yes, this is sometimes derisively called "monkey patching," and it's not always a good idea.)

Your Turn 1

➤ a. Employee: Create a class Employee with a getter name and a property age. Make an Employee object and try to change its name.

➤ b. Increment: Create a class Increment with a property amount and two versions of a method increment: one that adds 1 to amount, and another that adds a value, inc_amount.

Applying Inheritance

As in all object-oriented languages and much the same as in Ruby, Crystal provides for single *inheritance*, indicated by: subclass < superclass. Putting properties and methods common to several classes into a superclass lets them all share functionality. That way, you can use all instance variables and all methods of the superclass in the subclass, including the constructors. You can see this in the following example where PDFDocument inherits initialize, name, and print from Document:

```
classes_and_structs/inheritance.cr
class Document
  property name

  def initialize(@name : String)
  end

  def print
    puts "Hi, I'm printing #{@name}"
  end
end

class PDFDocument < Document
end

doc = PDFDocument.new("Salary Report Q4 2018")
doc.print # => Hi, I'm printing Salary Report Q4 2018
```

You can also override any inherited method in the subclass. If the subclass defines its own initialize method(s), they aren't inherited anymore. If you want to use the superclass functionality after you overrode it, you can call any method of the superclass with super:

```
classes_and_structs/inheritance.cr
class PDFDocument < Document
  def initialize(@name : String, @company : String)
  end

  def print
    super
    puts "From company #{@company}"
  end
end

# doc = PDFDocument.new("Salary Report Q4 2018")
# => Error: wrong number of arguments for 'PDFDocument.new' (given 1,
# => expected 2)
doc = PDFDocument.new("Salary Report Q4 2018", "ACME")
doc.print

# => Hi, I'm printing Salary Report Q4 2018
#    From company ACME
```

Crystal's type system gives you more options here. Instead of overriding, you can define specialized methods by using type restrictions, such as print in PDFDocument:

```
classes_and_structs/inheritance.cr
class PDFDocument < Document
  def initialize(@name : String, @company : String)
  end

  def print(date : Time)
    puts "Printing #{@name}"
    puts "From company #{@company} at date #{date}"
  end
end

doc = PDFDocument.new("Salary Report Q4 2018", "ACME")
doc.print(Time.now)

# => Printing Salary Report Q4 2018
#    From company ACME at date 2017-05-25 12:12:45 +0200
```

Using Abstract Classes and Virtual Types

Ruby doesn't have native support for interfaces and abstract classes like Java or C#. In both Ruby and Crystal, the concept of an interface is implemented through modules, as you'll see in the next chapter. But Crystal also knows the concept of an abstract class, so if you're a Rubyist, the following will be new to you.

Not all classes are destined to produce objects, and abstract classes are a good example. These serve instead as a blueprint for subclasses to implement their methods. Here you see a class, Rect (describing rectangles), forced to implement all abstract methods from class Shape:

classes_and_structs/inheritance.cr
```
abstract class Shape
  abstract def area
  abstract def perim
end

class Rect < Shape
  def initialize(@width : Int32, @height : Int32)
  end

  def area
    @width * @height
  end

  def perim
    2 * (@width + @height)
  end
end

s = Shape.new        # => can't instantiate abstract class Shape
Rect.new(3, 6).area # => 18
```

If one of the methods (say perim) isn't implemented, the compiler issues an error like the following:

```
error: "abstract `def Shape#perim()` must be implemented by Rect"
```

This lets you create class hierarchies where you can be confident that all necessary methods are implemented.

You can create more intricate structures as well. In the following example, class Document is called a *virtual type* because it combines different types from the same type hierarchy—in this case, different documents:

classes_and_structs/virtual.cr
```
class Document
end

class PDFDocument < Document
  def print
    puts "PDF header"
  end
end

class XMLDocument < Document
  def print
    puts "XML header"
  end
end
```

```
class Report
  getter doc

  def initialize(@name : String, @doc : Document)
  end
end

salq4 = Report.new "Salary Report Q4", PDFDocument.new
taxQ1 = Report.new "Tax Report Q1", XMLDocument.new
```

This virtual type is indicated by the compiler as type Document+, meaning that all types inherit from Document, including Document itself. It comes into play in situations like the one that follows where you'd expect d to be of a union type (PDFDocument | XMLDocument):

```
if 4 < 5
  d = PDFDocument.new
else
  d = XMLDocument.new
end
typeof(d) # => Document
```

Instead, d is of type Document. Internally the compiler uses this as a virtual type Document+ instead of the union type (PDFDocument | XMLDocument), because union types quickly become very complex in class-hierarchies.

If you call a method in a subclass of Document, you get an error:

```
salq4.doc.print # => Error: undefined method 'print' for Document
```

To remove this error, simply make the class Document abstract.

classes_and_structs/virtual.cr
```
abstract class Document
end

salq4.doc.print # => PDF header
```

Your Turn 2

➤ Shape: Subclass Shape with classes Square and Circle. (Hint: Use PI from the Math module with: include Math.)

Controlling Visibility

Objects that are visible can be read or even changed through external code, which is a common cause of bugs and surprises. Restricting this visibility, *encapsulating* your code, is very common in object-oriented languages.

It all centers around the concept of a *namespace* in code—an area in the code that's defined by a name. A class is a simple example: everything inside the class definition forms part of its namespace. By default, an object is visible in the whole namespace in which it's defined: it's *public* within that namespace, but not visible outside that namespace. We'll talk about this in more detail in the next chapter about modules.

In Crystal, methods are public by default. That is, they're usable inside and outside the class where they're defined. To restrict visibility, you can prefix the method definition with either private (the name says it all) or protected.

Making Methods Private

Private methods are more like helper methods: you can only use them inside a class or its subclasses, and they can't be called on an object.

```
classes_and_structs/private.cr
class Document
  property name

  def initialize(@name : String)
  end

  private def print(message)
    puts message
  end

  def printing
    print "Hi, I'm printing #{@name}"
    # self.print "Printing with self does not work"
    # => Error: private method 'print' called for Document
  end
end

class PDFDocument < Document
  def printing
    super
    print "End printing PDFDocument"
  end
end

doc = Document.new("Salary Report Q4 2018")
doc.printing # => Hi, I'm printing Salary Report Q4 2018

pdoc = PDFDocument.new("Financial Report Q4 2018")
pdoc.printing # =>
# Hi, I'm printing Financial Report Q4 2018
# End printing PDFDocument
# doc.print("test") # => Error: private method 'print' called for Document
```

Types like enums can also be private. Then you can only use them inside the namespace in which they're defined. In the same way, you can use only top-level methods or types that are marked private in the current code file. You can also use private with classes, modules, and constants, as well as aliases and libs, which you'll see later in the chapter.

Protecting Methods

Protected methods are a bit more subtle: they can do the same things as their private siblings, but they can also be called on an object. This object must be of the same type as the current type, for example, the class we're in, or in the same namespace. Here's an example to make this more concrete:

```
classes_and_structs/protected.cr
class Document
  property name

  def initialize(@name : String)
  end

  protected def print(message)
    puts message
  end

  def printing
    print "Hi, I'm printing #{@name}"
    self.print("This works too: self is a Document")
    doc = Document.new("Taxes")
    doc.print("This also: doc is a Document")
  end
end

class BankAccount < Document
  def printing
    doc = Document.new ("TestDoc")
    doc.print "inside BankAccount"
  end
end

class BankAccount2
  def printing
    doc = Document.new ("TestDoc")
    doc.print "inside BankAccount2"
  end
end

doc2 = Document.new "Audit 2017"
doc2.printing
# => Hi, I'm printing Audit 2017
# => This works too: self is a Document
# => This also: doc is a Document
doc2.print "Audit" # => Error: protected method 'print' called for Document
ba = BankAccount.new "test"
ba.printing # => inside BankAccount
ba2 = BankAccount2.new
# ba2.printing # => Error: protected method 'print' called for Document
```

The protected print method works inside class BankAccount because it's a subclass of Document and so it lives in that namespace. It doesn't work inside class BankAccount2 because that's outside of the namespace of class Document, resulting in an:

```
error: protected method 'print' called for Document.
```

Overloading Operators

The overloading you saw in the previous exercise also works for operators. The following code snippet shows overloading the operator ==. Let's say that two Mineral specimens are equal when they have the same ID. They must both be Minerals, so we use self here as a type-restriction. The same logic is expressed in the class method compare:

```
classes_and_structs/classes.cr
class Mineral
  getter id, name, hardness, crystal_struct
  property quantity : Float32

  def initialize(@id : Int32, @name : String, @hardness : Float64,
                 @crystal_struct : String)
    @quantity = 0f32
  end

  def ==(other : self) # self is Mineral
    id == other.id
  end

  def ==(other)
    false
  end

  def self.compare(m1 : self, m2 : self)
    m1.id == m2.id
  end
end

m1 = Mineral.new(101, "gold", 1.0, "cubic")
m2 = Mineral.new(108, "gold", 1.0, "cubic")
m3 = Mineral.new(101, "gold", 1.0, "cubic")
m1 == m2                  # => false
m1 == m3                  # => true
Mineral.compare(m1, m2) # => false
```

Note that the Ruby syntax class << self for class methods doesn't exist in Crystal. Class methods are methods prefixed with self..

Now ask yourself: can a class have multiple initialize methods? (In Ruby, the answer is no.)

Yes, it can—this is possible because of overloading. Here's an example to convince you:

```
classes_and_structs/classes.cr
class Mineral
  getter id, name, hardness, crystal_struct
  property quantity : Float32

  def initialize(@id : Int32, @name : String, @hardness : Float64,
                 @crystal_struct : String)
    @quantity = 0f32
  end

  def initialize(@id : Int32)
    @quantity = 0f32
    @name = "rock"
    @hardness = 0
    @crystal_struct = "unknown"
  end
end

m1 = Mineral.new(101, "gold", 1.0, "cubic")
m4 = Mineral.new(42)
# => #<Mineral:0x271bd40
# @crystal_struct="unknown",
# @hardness=0,
# @id=42,
# @name="rock",
# @quantity=0>
```

The Program

In Ruby, the top-level program is an instance called main of class Object:

```
# Ruby code!
puts self          # main
puts self.class    # Object
```

If we treat this as Crystal code, we get a compiler error: "there's no self in this scope". But inside a class, self is the class name. Inside an instance method, self is the current instance, as in Ruby:

```
classes_and_structs/program.cr
def display
  puts "Top-level display"
end

class Mineral
  puts self # => Mineral
  getter name
  getter hardness
  getter crystal_struct
```

The Program

```
    def initialize(@name : String, @hardness : Float64,
                   @crystal_struct : String)
    end

    def display
      ::display # => Top-level display
      p self    # => <Mineral:0x271cf00 @crystal_struct="cubic",
      #          @hardness=1.0, @name="gold">
    end
  end

  min1 = Mineral.new("gold", 1.0, "cubic")
  min1.display
```

To invoke a top-level method, such as display, in a method inside a class, prefix it with ::. Crystal has no main, but rather a kind of anonymous top-level namespace called the Program where methods such as puts, p, raise, spawn, and others, as well as some macros, live.

A Crystal program is a namespace in which you can define (and call) methods, types, constants, file-local variables, classes, and so on.

Working with Structs

Objects created from classes take up heap memory, and the garbage collector needs to release that. As you saw in the loop code in *Structuring a Class*, on page 96, creating many objects can quickly consume a lot of resources. To boost performance in such a case, you can use a sort of lightweight class called struct, which inherits from class Struct.

Structs are allocated in stack memory, so a struct is copied when reassigned or passed to a method. In other words: it's passed by value. At first sight, they look very much like classes: they have properties, constructors, and methods, and they can even be generic.

The following example defines a struct to accommodate user data:

classes_and_structs/structs.cr
```
struct User
  property name, age

  def initialize(@name : String, @age : Int32)
  end

  def print
    puts "#{age} - #{name}"
  end
end
```

```
d = User.new("Donald", 42)
d.name # => Donald
d.age = 78
d.print # => 78 - Donald
```

Changing Structs in Methods

Because structs are copied when passed, you must think about returning the value and reassigning it after return. In the following snippet, the no_change method doesn't change the struct, only the change method works:

classes_and_structs/structs.cr
```
def no_change(user)
  user.age = 50
end

def change(user)
  user.age = 50
  user
end

d = User.new("Donald", 78)
d.print # => 78 - Donald
no_change(d)
d.print # => 78 - Donald
d = change(d)
d.print # => 50 - Donald
```

Structs work best for non-changing (also called *immutable*) data structures, especially when the structure is small and you have lots of them. As a good example, the standard library implements complex numbers through the struct Complex.

Inheritance can also be defined for a struct, but only from an abstract struct.

Use Structs for Performance

Try changing class to struct in your code and see if it enhances performance. If it does and it fits with the functionality, go for it.

Your Turn 3

➤ Vec2D—Overloading an Operator on a Struct: Suppose you need to add lots of two-dimensional vectors. Define a struct Vec2D for doing just that and overload the + operator. Then define a few of them and work with these vectors. (Hint: Restrict the + operation to adding another Vec2D by using self.)

Viewing the Type Hierarchy

By now, you probably suspect that there's an entire *class hierarchy* at work behind every Crystal program. It can even be visualized with the *crystal hierarchy tool*. For example:

```
$ crystal tool hierarchy virtual.cr
```

shows all classes and structs from your program as well as the standard library. If you only want a fragment of that tree, your own classes for example, use the -e flag:

```
$ crystal tool hierarchy -e Document virtual.cr
```

This produces the following output:

```
- class Object (4 bytes)
  |
  +- class Reference (4 bytes)
     |
     +- class Document (4 bytes)
        |
        +- class PDFDocument (4 bytes)
        |
        +- class XMLDocument (4 bytes)
```

Let's make a schema for the most important types, which includes classes as well as structs (for example Int32), that can be abstract or not. Each indentation corresponds to a new subclass level as shown in the figure on page 110.

The ultimate superclass is, of course, Object, from which every object inherits lots of methods, such as == and to_s. Then we have a sharp distinction between the objects in the branch inheriting from Value, which are created in stack memory, and the branch inheriting from Reference, which are allocated in heap memory.

Stack memory is much faster to allocate than heap memory, and doesn't need to be garbage collected, but all values are copied and memory is limited. Heap memory lets a program pass around references instead of values, and is automatically garbage collected. Heap memory is typically used for things like arrays that need to grow dynamically. An Exception is also a heap object.

You can give a type or a group of types a synonym name with alias, as was done here to define a shorter name:

classes_and_structs/types.cr
```
alias PInt32 = Pointer(Int32)
```

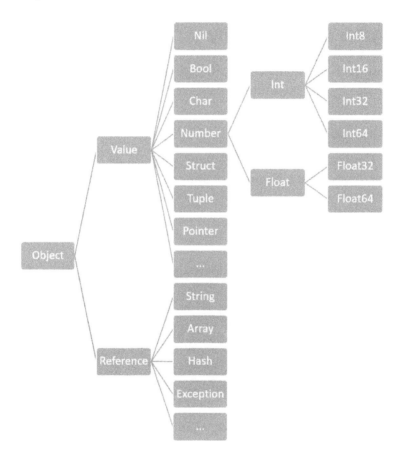

Some Nice Tricks

Now that you know the foundations of how Crystal's classes and structs work, it's time to explore some things that make it easier to use them.

to_s(io)

A convenient class should have a method that converts its objects to a string in order to describe itself. A Java developer will know this as the toString() method. A Rubyist will know to_s, which is inherited from Object. Crystal also knows to_s.

However, it's best not to use this form, but rather to override the to_s(IO) method. From the previous section, you know that a String is created in heap memory: if you need to create lots of them, that will damage your program's performance because they all have to be garbage collected. You should avoid creating too many temporary strings or objects in general. Instead, append your objects with << immediately to an IO object, without creating intermediate strings through interpolation, using to_s or concatenation, as in the first of the to_s methods that follow:

classes_and_structs/useful.cr
```
class Mineral
  getter name, hardness

  def initialize(@name : String, @hardness : Float64)
  end

  # Good
  def to_s(io)
    io << name << ", " << hardness
  end

end

min1 = Mineral.new("gold", 42.0)
io = IO::Memory.new
# To see what io contains, use to_s:
min1.to_s(io).to_s # => "gold, 42.0"
```

IO is a module for input and output in Crystal, supporting many different media: in memory, on a file, on a socket, and so on.

Using Exception as a Class

Knowing that Exception is a class, you can infer that it has a lot of subclasses, such as IndexError, TypeCastError, IO::Error, and others. In addition, you can also define your own subclasses:

```
class CoolException < Exception
end

raise CoolException.new("Somebody pushed the red button")
# => Somebody pushed the red button (CoolException)
```

Better rescue this! You can use multiple rescue branches, which each accept a certain type of Exception, putting a catchall rescue branch at the end:

classes_and_structs/useful.cr
```
ex = begin
  raise CoolException.new
rescue ex1 : IndexError
  ex1.message
rescue ex2 : CoolException | KeyError
  ex2.message
rescue ex3 : Exception
  ex3.message
rescue # catch any kind of exception
  "an unknown exception"
end # => "ex2"
```

Here's a more realistic example of exception handling when reading a file, trying to parse it in JSON format, and then writing it back to another file:

```
classes_and_structs/useful.cr
require "json"
path = "path/to/file"

begin
  if File.exists?(path)
    raw_file = File.read(path)
    map = JSON.parse(raw_file)
    File.write(path, "ok")
    :ok
  end
rescue JSON::ParseException # Parsing error
  raise "Could not parse file"
rescue ex
  raise "Other error: #{ex.message}"
end
```

Defining Callbacks

Using the concepts from *Working with Yield, Procs, and Blocks*, on page 74 about procs, here's a nice way to define a series of callbacks. A callback is a method that has to be called when a certain event happens. In this case, each after_save call adds a new callback, and when the save event finally occurs, each one of the callbacks in turn is called:

```
classes_and_structs/useful.cr
class MineralC
  def initialize
    @callbacks = [] of ->
  end

  def after_save(&block)
    @callbacks << block
  end

  # save in database, then execute callbacks
  def save
    # save

  rescue ex
    p "Exception occurred: #{ex.message}"
  else
    @callbacks.each &.call
  end
end
```

```
min = MineralC.new
min.after_save { puts "Save in DB successful" }
min.after_save { puts "Logging save" }
min.after_save { puts "Replicate save to failover node" }
min.save # =>
# Save in DB successful
# Logging save
# Replicate save to failover node
```

Your Turn 4

➤ a. Reopen a Class:

By now, you know why the following code gives an exception:

```
x = rand < 0.0001 ? 1 : "hello"
x - 1 # => Error: undefined method '-' for String
```

Define a new method for String by overloading the - operator. It should take a number and cut off as many characters from the string as the number indicates.

➤ b. Reopen a Method:

Predict what the p statements in the following code will show, first in Crystal and then in Ruby. Try it out and explain the difference:

```
class A
  def b
    41
  end
end
# this can also be written on 1 line as: class A; def b; 41; end; end;

p A.new.b

class A
  def b
    42
  end
end

p A.new.b
```

A method can be redefined and effectively overwritten, but you can invoke the earlier version inside the redefinition with previous_def.

A Company's Story Crystallized: LI-COR Biosciences

Nick Franken is a developer at LI-COR Biosciences,[1] an international company that designs and manufactures biological and environmental research equipment. It is based in Nebraska, USA. Nick has been using Crystal at LI-COR for about a year now. He is also the creator of *Crecto* (a database wrapper for Crystal) and core team member/contributor to the *Amber* web framework.

Ivo: *What production projects do you use Crystal for?*

Nick Franken: *We are using Crystal at LI-COR Biosciences for several projects: an authentication and account service used to authenticate and handle Stripe payments for LI-COR software products, a websocket service to handle messaging between environmental research instruments and web servers, and a websocket service, for a live collaborative lab classroom notebook used at various universities, including the University of Nebraska at Lincoln.*

Ivo: *Why did you decide to use Crystal for these applications?*

Nick Franken: *Crystal seems like an obvious choice for me for most projects. There are instances, though, where Python would be chosen instead, mostly where scientific libraries are needed that do not exist yet in Crystal.*

If Crystal hadn't existed, the alternative probably would have been Ruby or Python. As a science-based company, Python is the primary language used for many projects at LI-COR because of the many scientific libraries.

Ivo: *What was it like to develop with Crystal?*

Nick Franken: *My background is with Ruby, which made learning Crystal very easy and very enjoyable. I've heard others say this, and the same is true for me: programming in Crystal is the most fun I've had in a long time. It's the same type of fun I experienced when first learning Ruby.*

Crystal still lacks maturity, both in the standard library and external shards (these are Crystal's packages). This can make development harder if a certain shard does not exist, whereas with more mature languages, more libraries are already built.

Ivo: *Are there any aspects of Crystal that specifically benefit customer satisfaction?*

Nick Franken: *Single binary compilation makes deployment EXTREMELY easy, compared to deploying an application in Ruby on Rails or Python Django. For me personally, this gives Crystal a huge advantage when deciding between web frameworks.*

Ivo: *What advantages or disadvantages have you experienced when deploying a Crystal application in production?*

---

1.   https://www.licor.com/

Nick Franken: *One advantage when deploying a web application is the http server that is built into the application. Proxy and intermediary servers are not needed, whereas with a Rails application one might need Nginx and Unicorn.*

The application also consumes WAY less system resources than a Ruby application. Sometimes a 512MB server was too small to deploy a Rails app, where a similar sized Crystal application will utilize maybe 5 percent of this.

In my experience so far, request times are considerably lower than a similar Ruby, Python or even Node.js application.

Ivo: *What do you like the most about Crystal, compared to other languages?*

Nick Franken: *Static typing combined with compilation to a single binary, and the speed, and Ruby syntax.*

Wrapping Up

Classes, hierarchies, and method overloading should no longer be mysterious. Use visibility restrictions with private and protected, or inherit from normal and abstract types to tighten your code. Structs can give a performance benefit in certain situations.

In the next chapter, we'll look at modules, which structure code even at a higher level.

## CHAPTER 6

Working with Modules

When you're first learning a language, most simple examples fit in one file. As you embark on real projects, though, you need a way to group different code files and keep your code from tangling. This chapter and the next will show you the techniques you need to build maintainable large-scale Crystal projects.

Combining Files with Require

Until now, we've been putting all of our code into one source file, which works well for small examples. When code size grows and you need multiple classes, though, you'll want to split your code over several files. You can combine these into one file with require, which takes the following format:

```
require "path"
```

Here, path is the file-path to the file (or files) you want to include. When the compiler sees a require, it searches the file(s) on that path and copies in their contents in the present file. In this way, all source files are combined into one big file. This is only done once: a subsequent require of a previously required file will have no effect.

There are several forms of this command, which can make it a bit confusing at first. We'll illustrate them one by one.

In this demonstration, each required file prints out a statement that says where it's located. The code download contains everything, but this is what the folder and file structure look like:

- fileA.cr
- dirA
    - dirB.cr
    - fileA.cr

- fileA2.cr
- fileA3.cr
- dirB
  - dirB.cr
  - fileB.cr
- dirC
  - fileC1.cr
  - fileC2.cr

Looking in the Current Folder

The require "./part" form searches for part.cr or, if this wasn't found, part/part.cr (here part/ is a subfolder) in the current folder. Here are some examples:

working_with_modules/require.cr
```
require "./fileA"
# I am from fileA.cr in the current folder
# OR (if present): fileA.cr in subfolder fileA
require "./dirA/fileA"
# I am from fileA.cr in dirA
require "./dirA/dirB"
# I am from dirB.cr in dirA
# OR: I am from dirB.cr in dirB in dirA
```

To make it easy to see the difference, you can explicitly use require "./part.cr" when a file is intended.

Looking in the Parent Folder

Adding an extra period to make it require "../part" works like the previous form, except that now the compiler looks in the parent folder.

working_with_modules/require.cr
```
require "../fileA"
# I am from fileA.cr in the parent folder
require "../dirA/fileA"
# I am from fileA.cr in dirA in the parent folder
```

You can go up several levels as well, as in require "../../part".

Looking Several Levels Down

Nested forms also work, as you see here:

working_with_modules/require.cr
```
require "./dirA/dirB/fileB"
# I am from fileB.cr in dirB in dirA
```

Wildcards for Files or Subfolders

Using wildcard *: require "./dirA/*" looks for all .cr files in the dirA folder but not in subfolders.

working_with_modules/require.cr
```
require "./dirA/*"
# I am from fileA2.cr in dirA
# I am from fileA3.cr in dirA
```

If you also want to look in subfolders with a wildcard, you can use require "./dirA/**". This looks for all .cr files in the dirA folder, and also in subfolders, like dirC.

working_with_modules/require.cr
```
require "./dirA/**"
# I am from fileC1.cr in dirC in dirA
# I am from fileC2.cr in dirC in dirA
```

Using Crystal's Folder Structures

You can also bring in files using Crystal's *require path* with require "file".

working_with_modules/require.cr
```
require "file"
```

This looks up file.cr or file/file.cr in the require path, which consists of two parts.

The first is the location of the *standard library*, which in Linux is at /opt/crystal/src. You won't put anything here, but the compiler needs it to locate all Crystal source files.

The second is a lib folder relative to the current working folder. As you build larger projects, the reliable structure this approach offers will be appealing. You'll use this form to include external libraries in a project. In the next chapter, you'll see how the default project structure uses these rules.

Prelude

 Ever wondered why you don't need to require code for working with Booleans, chars, strings, arrays, and all such common types and modules? That's because they're all required in the prelude script, which you can often find on Linux at /opt/crystal/src/prelude.cr, or wherever your Crystal installer put it. You can also find the latest version of prelude.cr in the GitHub repository.[1]

---

1. https://github.com/crystal-lang/crystal/tree/master/src

Using Modules as Namespaces

Different libraries sometimes use the same names for methods or variables, leading to unwanted collisions. To distinguish these from each other, you need an additional name—the name of the module the object is defined in.

Modules structure code by defining namespaces. You can use a module to contain a complete implementation of related functionality, including constants, methods, classes, and even other modules. You saw a first example in *Organizing Code in Classes and Modules*, on page 34. Here's another one:

```
working_with_modules/namespaces.cr
module Crystals
  class Rhombic
  end

  class Triclinic
  end
end

t = Crystals::Rhombic.new
typeof(Crystals) # => Class
```

Note the namespace notation :: in Crystals::Rhombic.new. You see that the type of a module is Class. But can you make an object out of a Module? Try it out before going further.

Now you can see how a name clash (two or more methods with the same name that exist in different modules) is resolved. The fact a module is a namespace helps you avoid the clash: you can prefix the synonym method names with the module name, as in Module.method, so the compiler never sees ambiguity. In fact, as a library writer, you *should* always use a module to avoid that problem.

Here's another, slightly perverse, illustration:

File trig.cr defines a module Trig for some trigonometric calculations, in particular the sin function.

```
working_with_modules/trig.cr
module Trig
  PI = 3.141592654

  def self.sin(x)
    puts "Calculating the sin of #{x}"
  end

  def self.cos(x)
    # ..
  end
end
```

Our example also needs to make moral judgments (yes, a strange combination). So in file moral.cr, we have a module Moral with also a sin method.

working_with_modules/moral.cr

```
module Moral
  VERY_BAD = 0
  BAD      = 1

  def self.sin(badness)
    puts "Assessing the sin of #{badness}"
  end
end
```

Top-level methods in modules are like class methods (see *Structuring a Class*, on page 96)—they're prefixed with self. and are called as Module.method.

Let's use require to structure the code in another file:

working_with_modules/namespaces.cr

```
require "./trig"
require "./moral"

y = sin(Trig::PI/4)                    # => Error: undefined method 'sin'
y = Trig.sin(Trig::PI/4)               # => Calculating the sin of 0.7853...
wrongdoing = Moral.sin(Moral::VERY_BAD) # => Assessing the sin of 0
```

You see, you have to prefix the method name with the module name, like Trig.sin or Moral.sin, to satisfy the compiler.

Your Turn 1

➤ Use Built-in Sin: We couldn't resist the sin synonym, but in a real project, of course, you'd use the built-in Math module for calculating sine. Rewrite the code so that it uses this built-in sin method. (Hint: Because module Math is so commonly used, it needs no require. See math_sin.cr.)

The visibility rules you saw used for classes in the previous chapter also work here. You can, for example, use protected inside a module:

working_with_modules/visibility.cr

```
module Languages
  class Crystal
    protected def shout
      puts "Hello, I am written in Crystal"
    end
  end
```

```
  class Ruby
    def shout
      Crystal.new.shout
    end
  end
end
```

```
Languages::Ruby.new.shout # => Hello, I am written in Crystal
Languages::Crystal.new.shout
# => Error: protected method 'shout' called for Languages::Crystal
```

The first statement works because classes Crystal and Ruby live in the same namespace, Languages. But the second statement gives a compiler error because shout in the class Crystal is protected, so you can't use it directly as a top-level function.

Letting Modules Extend Themselves

The self. prefix for top-level methods can become a bit cumbersome. You can get rid of it by making a module extend itself:

working_with_modules/moral2.cr
```
module Moral
  extend self
  VERY_BAD = 0
  BAD      = 1

  def sin(badness)
    puts "Assessing the sin of #{badness}"
  end
end
```

You'll see this common idiom in modules—for example, module Math uses it in its code. When applied, a module is used as a namespace and you can write Module.method, like Math.sin. Now if this looks like a class method to you, it is! Remember: A module is of type Class.

working_with_modules/namespaces.cr
```
require "./moral2"

y = Math.sin(Math::PI/4)              # => 0.70710678118654746
wrongdoing = Moral.sin(Moral::VERY_BAD) # => Assessing the sin of 0
```

If you do an include of the module, you can even invoke its methods without a namespace as long as there's no ambiguity:

working_with_modules/namespaces2.cr
```
require "./moral2"
include Moral

y = Math.sin(Math::PI/4)        # => 0.70710678118654746
wrongdoing = sin(Moral::VERY_BAD) # => Assessing the sin of 0
```

Mixing in Modules

Modules group methods, and then you can use their functionality in different classes. To do that, the module's code is *mixed-in* to other types, as in Ruby or Dart. You do this with the keyword include. When a class does an include ModuleName, its objects can use the methods of the included module as their own methods! You saw an example in *Organizing Code in Classes and Modules*, on page 34.

Here's another example: Both classes DVD and BlueRay include the module Debug, so objects made of these classes can use its method who_am_i?

```
working_with_modules/mixins.cr
class Basic
  def initialize(@name : String)
  end

  def to_s
    @name
  end
end

module Debug
  def who_am_i?
    "#{self.class.name} (\##{self.object_id}): #{self.to_s}"
  end
end

class DVD < Basic
  include Debug
  # ...
end

class BlueRay < Basic
  include Debug
  # ...
end

dv = DVD.new("West End Blues")
br = BlueRay.new("Attack of the Martians")
dv.who_am_i? # => DVD (#40886016): West End Blues
br.who_am_i? # => BlueRay (#40885984): Attack of the Martians
```

See the use of \# here? This is for when you need a literal # sign in the output.

To use the module's methods on the class itself, you have to extend the module:

```
working_with_modules/mixins.cr
module DebugC
  def who_am_i?
    "#{self.class.name}: #{self.to_s}"
  end
end
```

```
class CD < Basic
  extend DebugC
  # ...
end

cd = CD.new("Bach's Cello Suites")
cd.who_am_i? # => Error: undefined method 'who_am_i?' for CD
CD.who_am_i? # => "Class: CD"
```

Modules can also contain abstract methods. Each class that includes them has to make its specific implementation for these methods. You'll see examples of this in the section *Applying Built-In Modules*, on page 125.

A class can include (and/or extend) many modules, thus importing various types of behavior, so this mechanism is a kind of *multiple inheritance*. But wait—doesn't that make this a recipe for name collisions?

No. The next section shows you why it isn't.

How the Compiler Finds Methods

With all these possible combinations of modules and classes, you may wonder how the compiler always finds the right method. This is the secret:

Each class (or type) has an *ancestor list*: a list of parent classes, starting with the superclass and ending with Object. The compiler looks up methods in this list, from the class itself to Object. If a method isn't found, you'll get a compile error like the following:

```
error: undefined method 'method_name' for 'class_name'
```

This is different from Ruby where you get a runtime NoMethodError.

What happens when modules are included in the class and a module has a method with the same name as a method in one of the parent classes? Modules are prepended into the ancestor list: the module's method takes precedence. Take a look at what happens in the following example:

```
working_with_modules/ancestors.cr
module M1
  def meth1
    41
  end
end

class C1
  def meth1
    42
  end
end
```

```
class D1 < C1
  include M1
end

class E1 < D1
end

E1.new.m1    # => Error: undefined method 'm1' for E1
E1.new.meth1 # => 41  # meth1 from module M1 is called
```

meth1 from module M1 will be called, and not meth1 from class C1. If you write out the ancestor list, it appears as follows: E1 is the ancestor of D1 which is the ancestor of M1 which is the ancestor of C1 which is the ancestor of Object.

Applying Built-In Modules

When inspecting the standard library code,[2] you can see that lots of the building blocks in there are actually modules. Let's take a quick look at some of them.

Using Comparable

Suppose you want to be able to order the objects of a type, using operators < and >=, but also ==. Would you define all these comparison operators yourself? Of course not, because the generic module Comparable(T) has already done this for you. By including this module, you get the operators for free. There's only one catch: Comparable has one abstract method that your class has to implement—the so-called "spaceship operator": abstract def <=>(other : T).

All other comparisons are defined using <=>. Your code must work like this: compare the current object's property against the other's property, and then return -1, 0, or 1, depending on whether the current object's property is less than, equal to, or greater than the other's property. Let's look at a concrete example where we compare Person objects on their age:

working_with_modules/comparable.cr
```
class Person
  include Comparable(Person)

  getter name, age

  def initialize(@name : String, @age : Int32)
  end

  def <=>(other : self)     # other must be of type self, which is Person
    if self.age < other.age # here self is the current Person object
      -1
```

---

2.   https://crystal-lang.org/api/latest/

```
    elsif self.age > other.age
      1
    else # == case
      0
    end
  end
end
```

Because <=> is also defined for numbers, we can shorten our code as follows:

working_with_modules/comparable.cr
```
def <=>(other : self) # other must be of type self, which is Person
  self.age <=> other.age
end
```

Be sure to look at the code in comparable.cr[3]—it's written entirely in Crystal itself! See the T? It says the module is *generic*: it works for any type T that implements <=>. That's why we had to write include Comparable(Person).

Using Enumerable

This module, when mixed in, gives collection types a large set of methods to query, search, and filter data. The only requirement is that the type implements an each method that returns the subsequent items in the collection using yield. This code snippet defines a class Sequence that contains all integers from 0 to a certain number @top. The class Sequence includes the module Enumerable:

working_with_modules/enumerable.cr
```
class Sequence
  include Enumerable(Int32)

  def initialize(@top : Int32)
  end

  def each
    0.upto(@top) do |num|
      yield num
    end
  end
end

seq = Sequence.new(7)
# using some methods of module Enumerable:
seq.to_a              # => [0, 1, 2, 3, 4, 5, 6, 7]
seq.select &.even?    # => [0, 2, 4, 6]
seq.map { |x| x ** 2 } # => [0, 1, 4, 9, 16, 25, 36, 49]
```

---

3.   https://github.com/crystal-lang/crystal/blob/master/src/comparable.cr

Working with Iterators

Most of the Enumerable methods return an array: they process the collection eagerly. That works well for small volumes of data but creates performance problems as the volume of information grows.

If the number of items in the collection is large and you don't need to process them all at once, you need a *lazy* alternative that doesn't get all the items at once. This is precisely what Iterator was made for. It includes Enumerable, but it redefines a lot of its methods. To implement Iterator, a class needs to code a next method. But you can also use the of class method with next, as in these examples:

```
working_with_modules/iterator.cr
n = 0
inc = Iterator.of do
  n += 1
  n
end

inc.next # => 1
inc.next # => 2
inc.next # => 3

n = 0
m = 1
fib = Iterator.of { ret = n; n = m; m += ret; ret }

fib
  .select { |x| x.even? }
  .first(10)
  .to_a # => [0, 2, 8, 34, 144, 610, 2584, 10946, 46368, 196418]
```

Although the Fibonacci series is infinite, only the items you need (the first 10) are calculated.

Your Turn 2

➤ How do you change the example comparable.cr if you want to compare persons on the alphabetical order of their names?

A Company's Story Crystallized: Diploid

Peter Schols is the CEO of Diploid,[4] a company based in Leuven, Belgium. Diploid provides services and software to hospitals and labs for diagnosing rare diseases using clinical genome analysis.

---

4. http://www.diploid.com/

Ivo: *What production projects do you use Crystal for?*

Peter Schols: *We are using Crystal for parts of Moon, the first software package to autonomously diagnose rare disease using artificial intelligence. Moon is being used by hospitals worldwide to diagnose patients with severe genetic conditions. The software requires the patient's symptoms, as well as his/her genome data. It will then come up with the most likely mutation to explain the patient's condition.*

Before Moon, geneticists had to manually filter and rank mutations using special software in order to reach a diagnosis. This process can take from several hours to up to several days. Moon does the filtering and ranking automatically and proposes a diagnosis within three minutes.

Moon has been written mostly in Ruby. We've chosen Ruby for several reasons: rapid development, expressive syntax, lots of available libraries, and a great ecosystem. All of this results in developer happiness and faster development cycles. But while Ruby is fast enough for most parts of Moon, it can be slow for the most performance critical areas of our codebase. That's why we evaluated Crystal, among others, and eventually decided to develop in Crystal.

Ivo: *Why did you decide to use Crystal for these applications?*

Peter Schols: *When looking for a language that we could use to replace performance-critical code in our Ruby codebase, we evaluated many options: Swift, Elixir, Go, and Crystal.*

We specifically evaluated performance, syntax, and ease-of-use. Performance was assessed using a small benchmark script that includes the performance-critical operations that are typical for genome analysis (mostly string operations). Go topped the performance list, followed by Crystal. Surprisingly, Ruby outperformed Swift.

Go clearly won the performance criterium. Performance is not everything, however: infrastructure is very cheap compared to developer time. While Go is an interesting language with a great concurrency model, it lacks in several other areas. Features that we take for granted in Ruby or other languages are not available in Go. Examples include operator overloading or keyword extensibility, as well as true OOP. Moving from Ruby to Go sometimes feels like ignoring 20 years of progress made in language design.

Crystal, as the second best performer, combines this still excellent performance with a very Ruby-like syntax. Given that the rest of our code base has been written in Ruby, it's a great match. Moreover, Crystal has a Go-like concurrency model, so it basically takes the best from the Ruby world (expressive syntax, full OOP) and combines it with the best of Go (concurrency model, performance).

Ivo: *What kinds of problems does Crystal solve best?*

Peter Schols: *Any problem that is currently being solved by Ruby, Python, Go, or Rust could potentially be solved in Crystal.*

Given its similarity to Ruby, web frameworks will be an important part of the Crystal ecosystem. However, Crystal has a lot of potential in other fields, too. Python is popular in data science, but it's far from the fastest language. With Crystal, data scientists could have the ease-of-use of Python/Ruby combined with the performance of C. These advantages could make Crystal very suitable for domains like bioinformatics, where performance is really important. As many people in the bioinformatics field don't have a formal CS/engineering background, having a language that is easy to learn is important as well. Crystal does very well on both fronts.

In addition, due to its expressive nature and low barrier to entry—traits it inherited from Ruby—Crystal is a great tool for general scripting and systems software.

The interview with Peter Schols of Diploid continues at the end of the next chapter, *A Company's Story Crystallized: Diploid—Part 2*, on page 146.

Wrapping Up

Modules enable you to organize your code with namespaces and make it easy to provide a single source of common functionality across classes. As your projects get bigger, you'll move from finding them useful to finding them necessary. Always use a module to envelop your project. Extract related method functionality to a module so that you can include and reuse it in many classes. Take some time to get acquainted with the modules that come with the standard library, both so you can reuse them and so you can model your own module use on their practice.

We'll apply this immediately in the following chapter, using the tools Crystal provides to generate and manage projects.

## CHAPTER 7

Managing Projects

In this chapter, you'll see how to use Crystal's project tool chain. You'll be able to handle the Crystal tools for creating, extending, testing, and documenting a project. You'll also want to manage your projects' performance, so we'll also take a look at benchmarking code. This suite of extra features provides the polish you need to create code other people will want to use—and will save you time in the long run, too!

Creating a Shard

Explore some Crystal projects on GitHub, such as the sentry tool[1] or the MongoDB driver.[2] You'll notice that they all have the same simple structure, which we'll dissect in a moment. This similarity isn't a coincidence: they were all created with the Crystal tool chain. When starting a brand new application, this tool generates a basic app directory structure on which to build your project. So Crystal projects, or *shards* as they're called, have a common structure—this makes it easy to explore their code.

The command to create a new project has the following structure:

```
$ crystal init TYPE NAME [DIR]
```

TYPE can be app (for an application) or lib (when writing a library). NAME is, of course, the name of the project. The optional DIR argument is the folder where your project template will be generated. As of this writing, the TYPE option only generates a different shard.yml: for an app, the *targets* section is added.

Let's try it out for an app named proj1:

```
$ crystal init app proj1
```

---

1. https://github.com/samueleaton/sentry
2. https://github.com/datanoise/mongo.cr

Explore the structure of the output this command generates:

```
$ crystal init app proj1
   create   proj1/.gitignore
   create   proj1/.editorconfig
   create   proj1/LICENSE
   create   proj1/README.md
   create   proj1/.travis.yml
   create   proj1/shard.yml
   create   proj1/src/proj1.cr
   create   proj1/spec/spec_helper.cr
   create   proj1/spec/proj1_spec.cr
Initialized empty Git repository in ~/proj1/.git/
```

It created a lot of connected parts:

- A folder with the application's name, here proj1.

- README and LICENSE files.

- A .travis.yml file that easily integrates with Travis for continuous integration.

- A shard.yml file for dependency management (much like Ruby's gemfile).

- A src folder to contain the app's source code.

- A spec folder to contain the app's tests.

- An initialized and empty Git repository to help you manage version control and publish your project on GitHub or similar sites.

- An .editorconfig file that specifies consistent whitespace handling for many editors that might encounter your code.

After adding external libraries (which we'll do in a moment), say lib1 and lib2, a more complete structure would look like this:

- proj1
    - bin
    - lib
        - lib1
            - lib1.cr
        - lib2
            - lib2.cr
    - src
        - proj1.cr
        - spec
            - proj1_spec.cr
            - spec_helper.cr

External libraries are kept in a lib folder. Any executables we need will live in the bin folder.

Let's explore the generated code. We see that a module with the project's name is created. proj1.cr is our main file, and it contains the following:

```
# TODO: Write documentation for `Proj1`
module Proj1
  VERSION = "0.1.0"

  # TODO: Put your code here
  puts "app proj1 is started"
end
```

We've added a puts to show some output when the app is run.

The spec folder for tests contains the file proj1_spec.cr, with its first line:

```
require "./spec_helper"
```

It searches for and will find the file spec_helper.cr, which contains this code:

```
require "spec"
require "../src/proj1"
```

The first line requires the spec part of the standard library. The second line requires the main project file proj1.cr. In order to test the application, it needs to have access to its code, right?

Now how do we run our application? In a terminal window, go to the folder proj1, and then type the following:

```
$ crystal src/proj1.cr
```

Crystal will navigate the pieces described above to run the application. You should see the text "app proj1 is started" displayed.

To create an executable, use this command:

```
$ crystal build src/proj1.cr.
```

This creates a binary file, proj1, in the proj1 folder, which can then be started with:

```
$ ./proj1 .
```

This combines all the many pieces you described into a single executable binary file. You can distribute this binary to wherever you want to execute your app. It does not rely on any other dependencies (go ahead and try it!). If it is for a real production app, build it with the --release flag to include optimizations.

Look up the source code of the Crystal MongoDB driver.[3] Analyze its project structure so that you understand all the require statements.

Your Turn 1

➤ Create a project, *mineral*, from scratch with crystal init and try to incorporate as much code as you can from the previous chapters, Chapter 2, *Crystal Foundations*, on page 19 and Chapter 5, *Using Classes and Structs*, on page 89.

Formatting Code

The best way to format and lay out your code has been an important (and not always friendly) question in every programming language since the dawn of coding. Learning from the success of Go's gofmt and Rust's Rustfmt, Crystal has its own built-in code formatter to format your code to the recommended coding style.[4] It automatically formats all .cr files in the current directory and even formats code samples included in documentation blocks. You apply it like this:

```
$ crystal tool format file.cr
```

If you omit a filename, it works on all source files in the folder. It's easy to forget it, though, so more and more text editors, such as Sublime Text, and IDEs, such as Visual Studio Code, include it and do the formatting automatically when you save the file. Try some weird code restructuring on a somewhat bigger code file (such as classes_and_structs/classes.cr), and see how the format tool restores its beauty.

Documenting a Project

You do document your code, don't you? Crystal makes that easy: it allows for easy docs in Markdown format. It has no special doc syntax apart from #, so all your comments are documentation. First, read through the guidelines.[5] Now let's add some doc comments to your *mineral* project (you did create the exercise, didn't you?). Here's an example:

```
managing_projects/mineral/src/mineral.cr
require "./mineral/*"

module Mineral
  puts "app mineral is started!"
```

---

3. https://github.com/datanoise/mongo.cr
4. https://crystal-lang.org/docs/conventions/coding_style.html
5. https://crystal-lang.org/docs/conventions/documenting_code.html

```
module Hardness
  def data
    mohs = {"talc" => 1, "gold" => 2.5, "calcite" => 3,
            "apatite" => 5, "corundum" => 9}
  end

  def hardness
    data[self.name]
  end
end
# Every Mineral has **hardness** (see the `Hardness` module).
#
# To create a standard rocky Mineral:
#
# ```
# min1 = Mineral.new(108)
# min1.to_s
# ```
#
# The above produces:
#
# ```text
# "This is a mineral with id 108 and is called rock"
# ```
#
# Checks the hardness with `#hardness`.
class Mineral
  include Hardness
  getter id, name
  setter crystal_struct

  # Creates a mineral with given parameters
  def initialize(@id : Int32, @name : String, @crystal_struct : String)
  end

  # Creates a mineral with name "rock", 0 hardness and "unknown" structure
  def initialize(@id : Int32)
    @name = "rock"
    @crystal_struct = "unknown"
  end

  # Prints out a description of this mineral
  def to_s
    puts "This is a mineral with id #{id} and it is called #{name} "
    puts "It has #{crystal_struct} as crystal structure"
  end

  # Returns object properties in csv-format
  def to_csv
    "#{id},#{name},#{hardness},#{crystal_struct}"
  end
```

```crystal
    def ==(other : self)
      id == other.id
    end

    def ==(other)
      false
    end

    # Returns crystal structure of this mineral
    def kind_of_crystal
      @crystal_struct
    end

    # :nodoc:
    class Helper # no docs are created for this class
    end          # neither for private or protected classes
  end
end
```

Crystal comes with a built-in documentation generator, which is also used for the language's own API.[6] To generate documentation for your project, start a terminal and go inside the project root folder. Then type the following:

`$ crystal docs`

This will create a doc folder containing your project's documentation website. Start it up with doc/index.html. We show part of the class Mineral page in the figure on page 137.

Use the flag keywords BUG, DEPRECATED, FIXME, NOTE, OPTIMIZE, and TODO in your docs. These flags help indicate to yourself or others what still has to be done.

Writing Tests with Spec

Now that we have a nicely formatted and documented project, let's see how to write tests for our code. Remember: A project with no tests is like a disaster waiting to happen. Tests ensure that your code works and you don't feel afraid to change your code because this won't break existing features. Tests also help others to see the details of how your project works.

Crystal includes a unit testing framework called spec, which is similar to RSpec from Ruby. A spec here means a set of unit tests that goes with a file of code—a file is tested with a corresponding _spec file.

---

6. https://crystal-lang.org/api/latest/

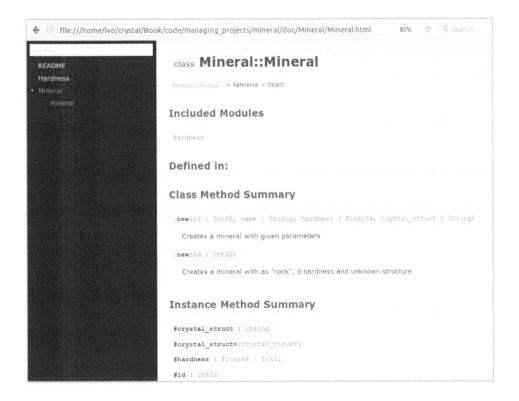

Let's look at the default mineral/spec/mineral_spec.cr (without the require statement):

```
describe Mineral do
  # TODO: Write tests

  it "works" do
    false.should eq(true)
  end
end
```

If you know Ruby, you will recognize describe, it, and should as keywords in the specs DSL:

- describe lets you group related specs.

- it is for defining a spec. Put its name between double quotes and the test code between do and end.

- should is for making assumptions about the spec.

These are all defined using the block syntax we visited in *Working with Yield, Procs, and Blocks*, on page 74.

We have one test named "works," which is obviously a placeholder and will fail. You can run the test by giving the following command in the project root folder:

$ crystal spec

Here's a screenshot:

```
ivo@ivo-SATELLITE-L50D-B:~/crystal/Book/code/managing_projects/mineral$ crystal
spec
app mineral is started!

Failures:

  1) Mineral works
     Failure/Error: false.should eq(true)

       Expected: true
            got: false

     # spec/mineral_spec.cr:7

Finished in 353 microseconds
1 examples, 1 failures, 0 errors, 0 pending

Failed examples:

crystal spec spec/mineral_spec.cr:6 # Mineral works
```

The difference between what we expected ("should") and what we found ("got") is signaled in red as an F for failure: the test "Mineral works" failed.

In general, all tests that are found are run. Every failed test produces an "F". For every successful test, you get a dot (.). To run only one test file, if you have several, give its name as an argument to crystal spec. To run one test, give its line-number nm like this:

$ crystal spec spec/file_spec.cr:nm

You can create as many tests as you like, as verbosely as you like, without affecting the final project performance. Tests aren't included in the generated project executable. Also, when you use spec without the --release flag, compile times are really fast and don't hamper development, even for bigger projects. Use the --release flag only when deploying your app. If you correct the failure in the placeholder test and compare the new output, you should see a green dot and the text "0 failures".

The code from the previous section that our new code will test is located in the spec folder, and now the test code requires the project's code. Let's write some tests for our mineral app.

We should test that the following works:

- Creating a mineral with the default parameters
- Creating a mineral with all parameters
- Generating CSV with the to_csv method
- Reading the hardness property from module Hardness
- Returning true with the == operator when comparing the same mineral
- Returning false with the == operator when comparing different minerals
- Getting the right value from the kind_of_crystal method

Here is code that tests these functionalities:

managing_projects/mineral/spec/mineral_spec.cr

```
require "./spec_helper"

describe Mineral do
  # TODO: Write tests

  # it "works" do
  #   false.should eq(true)
  # end

  it "creates a default mineral" do
    min1 = Mineral::Mineral.new(108)
    min1.id.should eq(108)
    min1.name.should eq("rock")
    min1.crystal_struct.should eq("unknown")
  end

  it "creates a mineral with parameters" do
    min1 = Mineral::Mineral.new(42, "apatite", "hexagonal")
    min1.id.should eq(42)
    min1.name.should eq("apatite")
    min1.crystal_struct.should eq("hexagonal")
  end

  it "creates correct csv format" do
    min1 = Mineral::Mineral.new(101, "gold", "cubic")
    min1.to_csv.should eq("101,gold,2.5,cubic")
  end

  it "gold has hardness 2.5" do
    min1 = Mineral::Mineral.new(42, "gold", "cubic")
    min1.hardness.should eq(2.5)
  end

  it "== works for same mineral" do
    min1 = Mineral::Mineral.new(42, "gold", "cubic")
    (min1 == min1).should eq(true)
  end
```

```
it "== works for different mineral" do
  min1 = Mineral::Mineral.new(42, "gold", "cubic")
  min2 = Mineral::Mineral.new(43, "corundum", "trigonal")
  (min1 == min2).should eq(false)
end

it "kind_of_crystal works" do
  min1 = Mineral::Mineral.new(42, "gold", "cubic")
  (min1.kind_of_crystal).should eq("cubic")
end
end
```

Go ahead and execute the specs and play with the test code.

Using External Libraries

When building your app, you don't want to reinvent the wheel. More often than not, parts of your functionality are already covered by existing Crystal packages or libraries. Commonly called *shards*, they're the equivalent of gems in the Ruby world.

shards is also the name of the application that manages the dependencies of a project, like bundler in Ruby. How can you instruct your app to load one or more external shards?

Your app can list its dependencies in the file shard.yml (for Rubyists: the gemfile), which we'll take a closer look at now. At the start of a project, it looks like this:

```
name: mineral
version: 0.1.0

authors:
  - Your-Name <your-email-address>

targets:
  mineral:
    main: src/mineral.cr

crystal: 0.22.0

license: MIT
```

It lists the startup file of the app, together with some general info. To add external packages, we need a new *dependencies* section.

Adding a Shard

Let's see how this works by adding a logging feature to our app, the katip logger developed by Güven Cenan. To keep our code short and clean, we'll work in a project mineral_log, which copies the code from project mineral.

There are two steps to add a shard to a project.

First, let's edit shard.yml in the root folder of mineral_log, add the following, and then save:

```
dependencies:
  katip:
    github: guvencenanguvenal/katip
```

Each external library is a dependency specified with its name and the link on GitHub to fetch its source code, so there's no need for a central Crystal repository. Beneath the link, you can also specify a specific version to use:

```
version: 0.1.2
```

Crystal won't typically change versions on you silently, but specifying the version explicitly may help other maintainers see what you did. If, on the other hand, you need the latest changes, use this:

```
branch: master
```

Next, you need to install the library and add it to the current project. Go to the root folder and do: $ crystal shards, or even shorter: $ shards.

This produces the following output:

```
Updating https://github.com/guvencenanguvenal/katip.git
Installing katip (version: 0.1.0)
```

If the shard you're adding also depended on other shards, they'll also be installed. You can see which shards were installed with:

```
$ shards list
```

which in our case produces:

```
Shards installed:
  * katip (0.1.0)
```

If you look inside the project structure, you can see what was created:

- A lib folder, containing a subfolder for each of the installed dependencies. Note that the source code is installed, not the executables.

- A hidden folder, .shards, containing a Git subfolder for each of the installed dependencies.

- A shard.lock text file, listing all of the installed shards and their version.

Changed Dependencies

The requirements of one of the dependencies might change, perhaps because you need other versions of the shards on which your app depends. Check this with $ shards check. If everything is okay, this gives the message: "Dependencies are satisfied." If not, run the command $ shards update.

Now that the shard is properly installed, you can start using it. First, you have to tell your app to load its code. Do this by adding the following at the start of src/mineral_log.cr:

```
require "katip"
```

As you saw in *Combining Files with Require*, on page 117, this will look for its source inside the lib folder.

Including the shard is just the start of the work to integrate it. Katip also needs some configuration code before it can run, like:

```
LOGGER = Katip::Logger.new

LOGGER.configure do |config|
  config.loglevel = Katip::LogLevel::DEBUG
  config.logclassification = Katip::LogClassification::DATE_DAY
  config.path = "src/katip/logfiles"
  config.info.description = "This is the Mineral Log project."
  config.info.project = "Mineral Log."
  config.info.version = MineralLog::VERSION # project version
end
```

Note how we create the logger object as a constant LOGGER, so we can access it in the module MineralLog and the class Mineral.

Now we're all set and done, and we can start adding logging messages—For example, at startup, when creating a Mineral object, when calling to_csv, and so on:

managing_projects/mineral_log/src/mineral_log.cr
```
module MineralLog
  LOGGER.info("app mineral_log is started!")

  min1 = Mineral.new(101, "gold", "cubic")
  puts min1.to_csv
end

class Mineral
  getter id, name
  property crystal_struct
```

```
  def initialize(@id : Int32, @name : String, @crystal_struct : String)
    LOGGER.debug("A new mineral is created!")
  end

  def initialize(@id : Int32, logger)
    @name = "rock"
    @crystal_struct = "unknown"
    LOGGER.debug("A new default mineral is created!")
  end

  def to_s
    puts "This is a mineral with id #{id} and is called #{name} "
    puts "It has #{crystal_struct} as crystal structure"
  end

  def to_csv
    LOGGER.debug("to_csv method is called")
    "#{id},#{name},#{crystal_struct}"
  end
end
```

Now you can find the logfile in src/katip/logfiles/*.json. Use the logviewer by starting up mineral_log/lib/katip/katipviewer.html in a browser:

Katip offers info, warn, debug, error, and fatal messages, so you can choose what to log and when to view it.

No Shared Dependencies

 In Crystal, each app has its own source copy of the shards on which it depends. These are compiled into the production executable. There are no shared dependencies, as long as the code is purely Crystal. This has several advantages:

- No dependency hell: no problems with shard versions out of sync! You know with which versions your app works, and shard.lock makes sure these versions are used.

- When you delete an app, you also delete all dependencies without leaving code behind.

- If there's a problem with a dependency, you can debug it and even change it without impacting other applications.

Benchmarking Your Code

Sometimes you need to investigate a performance problem on your app, or you want to see which is the fastest or more efficient of two possible algorithms. In that case, use the built-in Benchmark module, which takes minimal effort and provides great feedback. You may find it familiar if you've used its Ruby equivalent.

In *to_s(io)*, on page 110 in Chapter 5, you learned that appending a raw object is much faster than appending a string made by interpolation with #{} or to_s. Now that we're in a position to prove that, let's compare these three tasks. As you know by now, we work with IO::Memory objects to increase efficiency. Let's see how that goes:

managing_projects/benchmarking.cr
```
require "benchmark"

IOM = IO::Memory.new

Benchmark.ips do |x|
  x.report("Appending") do
    append
    IOM.clear
  end

  x.report("Using to_s") do
    to_s
    IOM.clear
  end
```

```
    x.report("Interpolation") do
      interpolation
      IOM.clear
    end
end

def append
  IOM << 42
end

def to_s
  IOM << 42.to_s
end

def interpolation
  IOM << "#{42}"
end
```

We require the Benchmark module to look it up in the standard library. Then we call the Benchmark.ips method, which measures iterations per second. Each task is enveloped in a do end block and is executed a large number of times to compare them. The task is called as a method, which is overkill here, but you'd do that in a real case. The report method then shows the results in a nice interface.

Build the code for production using $ crystal build benchmarking.cr --release and execute that with: $ ./benchmarking

You'll get results like this:

```
   Appending   34.06M ( 29.36ns) (± 3.97%)         fastest
   Using to_s  12.67M ( 78.92ns) (± 7.55%)  2.69× slower
Interpolation    2.8M (356.75ns) (± 3.84%) 12.15× slower
```

This proves our statement.

Also useful is the bm method, which shows you the time usage in report form:

```
managing_projects/benchmarking.cr
Benchmark.bm do |x|
  x.report("Appending bm") do
    IOM.clear
    10_000_000.times do
      append
    end
  end
end
```

```
                   user      system      total         real
Appending bm    0.240000    0.000000    0.240000 (  0.243686)
```

With this method, you have to specify the loop yourself.

Your Turn 2

➤ a. ArrayLastElem: To get the last element of an array, which method is the fastest: using -1 as index or last?

➤ b. Building_vs_Concat: In *Using String Methods*, on page 54 in Chapter 3, we also affirmed that string building is much more performant than concatenation. Prove this through benchmarking with bm. Use a string to concatenate or append to.

Deploying a Crystal App

When you're finished testing and benchmarking, you want to get your shiny app into production. This is easy: just distribute the binary!

Because everything needed is compiled in, there's only one executable file. Make sure before deployment to compile your app with the –release flag as described in *Compiling Code*, on page 195, which turns on optimizations.

A Company's Story Crystallized: Diploid—Part 2

Peter Schols is the CEO of Diploid,[7] a company based in Leuven, Belgium. Diploid provides services and software to hospitals and labs for diagnosing rare diseases using clinical genome analysis.

Ivo: *What was it like to develop with Crystal?*

Peter Schols: *When coming from Ruby, working in Crystal feels like coming home. Syntactically, Crystal is highly similar: the only major difference is the static typing. While this takes a bit to get used to, the transition was really smooth and easy. Many lines of code can literally be copied from a Ruby project and pasted into a Crystal project and they will just work. Some lines do need additional type annotations, however. Apart from that, the only major difference is that the rubygems (Ruby libraries) ecosystem is very expansive. Crystal has its own version of gems, called shards. While the number of shards has grown exponentially in the past few months, it's still way behind the rubygems ecosystem, or the Go ecosystem for that matter.*

Ivo: *Are there any aspects of Crystal that specifically benefit customer satisfaction?*

---

7.   http://www.diploid.com/

Peter Schols: *The Crystal code we use in production was not ported from Ruby; it was written from scratch in Crystal. However, in order to test the difference in performance—and also out of pure curiosity—we ported the code from Crystal to Ruby. For this particular project, we noticed that the Crystal version was 4.4x-6.1x faster.*

This made a big difference in user experience. It means that for smaller data sets, Moon can present results in near real time (about 540 ms), which feels instant to the user. The corresponding Ruby program takes 2.5 seconds for the same task. When analyzing larger data sets, the difference was even bigger: on average 27 seconds for Crystal compared to 2 minutes and 50 seconds for almost exactly the same Ruby code, a more than 6x speedup! When analyzing hundreds of samples, these time differences become even more important.

Ivo: *What advantages or disadvantages have you experienced from deploying a Crystal application in production?*

Peter Schols: *As mentioned, the speed increase is really significant. In addition, the ability to create a binary is convenient, as it allows for easy deployment.*

Compiling a binary also allows us to easily share software with our internal users and testers. With Ruby, we need to set up rvm or rbenv, install the latest Ruby version, install rubygems, and install all required gems. With Crystal, it's as easy as copying one file.

Ivo: *What do you like the most about Crystal, compared to other languages?*

Peter Schols: *Performance, the ability to create real binaries, and the Ruby-like syntax are the most important Crystal selling points for me.*

Another advantage is that Crystal makes it very easy to create bindings to a C library—no need to write C code.

Last but not least, Crystal has an amazing community of friendly and skilled developers. It started with Ary, Juan, and Brian at Manas, creating the language and helping the Crystal newbies. In the meantime, it seems like the entire community has copied their attitude of providing help and pointers to everyone who's interested in this very promising language.

More info about Moon is available here.[8]

Shown on page 148 is an image of the Moon software in action.

---

8.   http://www.diploid.com/moon

Wrapping Up

Congratulations! In this chapter, you stepped up from writing Crystal code to writing your own shard. Not only that but you now know how to standardize your code, document it, test it, benchmark it, and use shards from the Crystal world at large. In Part III, you'll extend your Crystal knowledge by learning how to write macros, access databases, and write concurrent code.

Part III

Advanced Crystal

In this part, we'll explore some advanced concepts in Crystal that you might need for production projects: using macros, concurrent execution, database access, and binding to C libraries. Many apps also need a web framework, and Crystal has powerful solutions in this area. We'll also look into the shard ecosystem.

## CHAPTER 8

Advanced Features

Now that you've seen the foundations of the Crystal language, let's explore features that you'll often need in real-life projects:

- *Macros* to avoid boilerplate code: Every modern programming language that respects itself can do this. Crystal respects itself and can do this.

- *Binding with C libraries*: Sometimes a good C library for your purposes already exists and you just want to use that. Crystal makes this easy: write out the C function names and types and you're good to go.

- *Concurrency*: Running different code parts at the same time. When applied with care, this improves throughput and performance, which is what we all want.

- *Database access*: Most apps need to store their data, so this is a no-brainer—you need this. Crystal proposes a unified way to do this.

These techniques will help you persist your app's data safely and boost its speed. You'll reuse functionality that already exists in C, and you'll make your code leaner and smarter by using metaprogramming. These topics aren't directly related, but applying them will take your Crystal coding to the next level.

DRY Your Code with Macros

Crystal's original inspiration, Ruby, is a master of runtime introspection and manipulation of code—also called *metaprogramming*. Metaprogramming is the secret to Ruby on Rails' sophistication, but Ruby has no macros. Crystal is a compiled language, so it doesn't have an eval method to create new code in runtime. It has to take a different path, a competent system of macros to build code at compile time, and that will go a long way.

When you're writing code, sometimes you'll find yourself writing methods that are near duplicates of each other, only differing in name or parameters. In these cases, it might help if you could generate all this code automatically using one macro version of the method.

A macro is a function that gets called while code is compiled. The output of the macro is more code, which gets compiled. Macros let you do more with less code.

Less code (usually) means fewer bugs. Don't repeat yourself—apply the DRY principle!

For example, let's see how we could implement a macro that returns the value of instance variables. We'll start from a simple Mineral class with attributes name and hardness, pretending we don't know about getter:

```
advanced_features/macros.cr
class Mineral
  def initialize(@name : String, @hardness : Float64)
  end

  def name
    @name
  end

  def hardness
    @hardness
  end
end

min1 = Mineral.new("gold", 2.5)
"#{min1.name} - #{min1.hardness}" # => "gold - 2.5"
```

Code is duplicated: for each attribute, we have a method of that name to return its value.

But we want something like this to use a new macro called get, right?

```
class Mineral
  def initialize(@name : String, @hardness : Float64)
  end

  get name
  get hardness
end
```

or even:

```
get name, hardness
```

Let's do this in steps:

1) First, copy the name method into a macro, get, like this:

advanced_features/macros.cr
```
macro get
  def name
    @name
  end
end

class Mineral
  def initialize(@name : String, @hardness : Float64)
  end

  get

  def hardness
    @hardness
  end
end

min1 = Mineral.new("gold", 2.5)
"#{min1.name} - #{min1.hardness}" # => "gold - 2.5"
```

The code still works: the macro, get, creates code for the method, name. A macro is defined like an ordinary method. But instead of def, the keyword macro is used.

2) Because we want this for every attribute, we must generalize the code:

advanced_features/macros.cr
```
macro get(prop)
  def {{prop}}
    @{{prop}}
  end
end

class Mineral
  def initialize(@name : String, @hardness : Float64)
  end

  get name
  get hardness
end

min1 = Mineral.new("gold", 2.5)
"#{min1.name} - #{min1.hardness}" # => "gold - 2.5"
```

The macro get now takes a parameter, prop, so we can use it for every attribute. The body of a macro often contains {{ }} expressions. These are *expanded* when code is generated from the macro at compile-time: every expression inside {{ }} is substituted in the generated code. So now we can use get for every attribute.

3) How can we reduce the code even more to get name, hardness? Because we don't know how many attributes there are, we use a splat * (see *Using the Splat Argument* *, on page 72). To loop over the attributes, we can use the following for in syntax:

```
{% for prop in props %}
  # code
{% end %}
```

The complete version looks like this:

advanced_features/macros.cr
```
macro get(*props)
  {% for prop in props %}
    def {{prop}}
      @{{prop}}
    end
  {% end %}
end

class Mineral
  def initialize(@name : String, @hardness : Float64)
  end

  get name, hardness
end

min1 = Mineral.new("gold", 2.5)
"#{min1.name} - #{min1.hardness}" # => "gold - 2.5"
```

The Crystal language includes many powerful built-in macros, such as getter, setter, and property, in a class definition. These aren't keywords. They are macros defined in class Object. There's even a record macro that can generate an entire struct definition for you:

advanced_features/macros.cr
```
record Mineral, name : String, hardness : Float64

min1 = Mineral.new("gold", 2.5)
"#{min1.name} - #{min1.hardness}" # => "gold - 2.5"
```

Macros are a great way for you to extend the language, even for writing DSLs (Domain Specific Languages).

Like the {% for in %} construct, there's a {% if %} {% else %}. You can use both outside of a macro definition as well. Inside a macro, you can access the current instance type with the special instance variable @type. Macros can live inside modules or classes. They can call each other, and a macro can even call itself recursively. Be careful, though—you need to define macros before you use them.

How do macros work? The compiler takes a few extra steps to generate the actual executable code. In the step that processes the Abstract Syntax Tree (AST), code using the macro syntax works on these AST nodes. These expand into valid Crystal code, which then compiles as usual. By hooking into the compilation process, you can do some sophisticated things, and it doesn't slow down runtime performance like it does in Ruby!

Your Turn 1

➤ def_method: Make a macro, define_method, that takes a method name, mname, and a body to construct that method. Test it by producing the code for a method, greets, that prints "Hi," and a method, add, that returns 1 + 2.

Hooking Up Macros

You might know from Ruby that you can generate code in runtime when a called method can't be found. You'd do this by defining a method_missing in the class. In Crystal, you can do something very similar with a macro, but here you generate the method at compile-time:

advanced_features/macros.cr
```
class Mineral
  getter name, hardness

  def initialize(@name : String, @hardness : Float64)
  end

  macro method_missing(call)
    print "Unknown method: ", {{call.name.stringify}},
          " with ", {{call.args.size}}, " argument(s): ",
          {{call.args}}, '\n'
  end
end

min1 = Mineral.new("gold", 2.5)
min1.alien_planet?(42)
# => Unknown method: alien_planet? with 1 argument(s): [42]
```

In the preceding example, the method alien_planet? doesn't exist in class Mineral. Normally, this would cause a compile error:

```
undefined method 'alien_planet?' for Mineral
```

With this macro, method_missing, in place, we have access to the method's name and arguments, coding something more useful than just printing them out.

In the same way, you can define the following macros, which are invoked at compile-time:

- inherited: When a subclass is defined, @type is the class that inherits.
- included: When a module is included, @type is the class that includes.
- extended: When a module is extended, @type is the class that extends.

Using these, you can program at a *meta*-level.

While macros are powerful, coding with macros is a lot more complicated. So, as a rule, don't use macros! If you really think you need a macro, first write the code without it, and check that you have duplicated code. If you do, then eliminate that by writing a macro. As you get deeper into macros, you will find more nuance and power in the docs.[1]

Low-Level Programming and C Bindings

Unlike Ruby, Crystal has a lot of features that make it useful for embedded and IoT applications. For example, you can work with pointers of any type, as you see here:

```
advanced_features/low_level.cr
ptr = Pointer(UInt8).malloc(20) # malloc allocates memory
ptr.value = 42_u8              # 42 here is of type u8
ptr                            # => Pointer(UInt8)@0x271dfe0
ptr.value                      # => 42
ptr.class                      # => Pointer(UInt8)

# Converting between pointer types with as:
# Int8* is the same as Pointer(Int8)
ptr.as(Int8*) # => Pointer(Int8)@0x271dfe0

n = 42
ptr_n = pointerof(n)
ptr_n.value = 108
n # => 108
```

A pointer does no checks at all: such code is regarded as *unsafe*, which means that memory corruption, segmentation faults, or other crashes could occur. You're on your own—the compiler doesn't help you out here. The Slice(T) type is like a pointer with a size—it does bound-checks, so it's safer to use than a Pointer. The often-used Bytes type is an alias for Slice(UInt8).

This openness may seem like odd behavior from the Crystal compiler, which usually protects you by setting strict limits. But this lets you explore the outer edges of programming, and it also makes it easier to interact with C

---

1. https://crystal-lang.org/docs/syntax_and_semantics/macros.html

code. Thanks to these features and Crystal's compiled nature, you can reuse a whole universe of C libraries that don't (yet) exist in Crystal without writing a single line of C. (You don't need to do this to gain speed: Crystal is on par with C in this regard.)

Binding to a C library is as easy as it can possibly get in Crystal, whereas in Ruby, you'd need to write C code. C is a strongly typed language, as is Crystal. That's why they can talk easily. As a first example, let's see how to call some common C functions from Crystal:

```
advanced_features/c_bindings.cr
lib LibC
  fun rand : UInt32
  fun sleep(seconds : UInt32) : UInt32
  fun atoi(str : UInt8*) : Int32
  fun printf(format : UInt8*, ...) : Int32
  fun cos(val : Float64) : Float64
  fun exit(status : Int32) : NoReturn
end

LibC.rand              # => 1804289383
LibC.sleep(1_u32)      # => wait 1 second
LibC.atoi("28").class  # => Int32

a = 1
b = 2
LibC.printf "%d + %d = %d\n", a, b, a + b # => 1 + 2 = 3
LibC.cos(1.5)                             # => 0.0707372016677029

LibC.exit(0) # => NoReturn
puts "hello" # this will never be executed
```

You see that the library itself is declared as lib LibC. The lib section groups C functions and types that belong to a certain C library—let's say nmo, which will be named LibNMO by convention in Crystal. Within this section, you declare the C functions you need as fun cfname. You must specify the name, argument type, and return type of these functions exactly as C expects. The C functions are then called in Crystal as class methods on the library, like LibC.atoi("28").

The previous example was particularly easy because LibC is defined in the standard library, and so it's implicitly linked. For other external libraries—for example, the SDL library used in writing computer games—you need to use an annotation @[Link("")] that can pass flags to the linker in order to find the library.

Types Used in C-Binding

You can use primitive types, such as Int8 to Int64, or their unsigned equivalents, or Float32 and Float64. You can also use Pointer types, like Pointer(Int32), which you can also write as Int32*.

The Void return type means the same as Nil in Crystal, and NoReturn means the end of execution.

The C char type is UInt8 in Crystal; LibC::Char is an alias. The Crystal Char type has 4 bytes, so to C, it's like an Int32. So a C pointer type like char* or a const char* is UInt8*.

---

advanced_features/c_libsdl.cr
```
@[Link("SDL")]
lib LibSDL
  INIT_TIMER = 0x00000001_u32
  INIT_AUDIO = 0x00000010_u32

  fun init = SDL_Init(flags : UInt32) : Int32
end

value = LibSDL.init(LibSDL::INIT_TIMER) # => 0
```

In this example, @[Link("SDL")] passes the flag -lSDL to the linker. You also see how you can make simple function names to use in Crystal, such as init instead of SDL_Init.

Let's now make a simple example to see how the linking works: greet.c contains a function greet, which says Hello to somebody.

advanced_features/greet.c
```
#include <stdio.h>

void greet(const char* name){
  printf("Hello %s!\n", name);
}
```

Compile this C code to an object file, greet.o, with $ gcc -c greet.c -o greet.o. Now in the Crystal code, we'll point the linker to where it can find the object file, as follows:

advanced_features/greet.cr
```
@[Link(ldflags: "#{__DIR__}/greet.o")]

lib LibSay
  fun greet(name : LibC::Char*) : Void
end

LibSay.greet("Ary") # => Hello Ary!
```

Compile and execute this as usual with $ crystal build greet.cr and $ ./greet to see the greeting.

Because using C bindings is inherently unsafe, it's best to write a safe wrapper around it that includes checks for nil pointers and index bounds. For many more details about interacting with C, look here.[2]

If you need to reach beyond Crystal's normal capabilities but all of C's possibilities are more than you need, Crystal can reach out to the operating system with the top-level system command, executing a given OS command in a subshell, as in this example, where gedit opens the file test.txt for editing:

```
file = "test.txt"
system("gedit #{file}")
```

It's simple, powerful, and exposes your code to all the same risks the operating systems has to offer. It also creates dependencies that you'll need to manage.

Creating Concurrent Code

For concurrent processing, Crystal uses the same CSP (communicating sequential processes) model as Go: lightweight processes called fibers that communicate data through channels. It does this faster and less resource-intensive than Node.js, for example. You learned about fibers and channels in Chapter 3, *Executing Code Concurrently Through Fibers*, on page 38. Before getting into more detail, let's examine Crystal's execution mechanism.

How Does a Crystal Program Execute?

When a Crystal program starts up, a main fiber (main for short) runs to execute your top-level code. In that code, one can spawn many other fibers, which are queued. In the background, Crystal operates a minimal runtime that consists of the following components:

1) A *Runtime Fiber Scheduler* takes care of executing all fibers in the queue at the right time. A fiber that can't proceed (because it's waiting for Input/Output) works cooperatively: it tells the scheduler to switch to another fiber to start or to resume work. The scheduler also coordinates channels to communicate data between fibers.

2) A non-blocking *Event Loop* is just another fiber. It's in charge of everything I/O related—asynchronous tasks, such as file reading; network packet

---

2. https://crystal-lang.org/docs/syntax_and_semantics/c_bindings/

sending; timers; and so on. It waits on time-consuming tasks to end, while other fibers execute at the same time.

3) A *Garbage Collector* (GC) cleans up memory that the program is no longer using. This is currently a standard mark-and-sweep Boehm GC.

You could describe a running Crystal program as a *cooperative multitasking* mechanism between any number of lightweight fibers, which allows for low overhead context switching. This works best for I/O intensive processing. It's a bit less adapted for CPU intensive processing, such as heavy number crunching.

Each fiber starts out with a stack size of 4KB, which can grow to a maximum of 8MB—the typical memory consumption of a thread. You can create lots of them if you need to, though you may find yourself limited on older hardware. On a 64-bit machine, you can spawn millions and millions of fibers. But on a 32-bit machine, you can only spawn 512.

All of this except the GC runs in one native OS thread. Up until the time of writing, Crystal has worked with only one execution thread, but real parallellism (as in Go) is coming soon. The GC runs in parallel, in a separate thread from the rest of the Crystal application.

The built-in scheduler means that you don't have to write the scheduling of fibers yourself. This might seem limiting, but it also means that you won't find yourself in callback hell as in Node.js with JavaScript. You just write your code as if it would execute in a linear order.

Establishing Channels Between Fibers

You know that a fiber is created with each `spawn do code end` line, where `code` will be executed by the new fiber. What do you think the following snippet will output?

```
advanced_features/main_fiber1.cr
puts "Before start fiber"
spawn do
  puts "Hello from within fiber"
end
puts "After fiber"
```

It will only output:

```
Before start fiber
After fiber
```

Why is this? The main fiber exits when the program ends, and with it, all the fibers it has spawned. When a fiber is spawned, it doesn't execute immediately. In this case, it never gets to show its message. We can remedy this by adding a sleep 1.second. Then the main fiber is halted for one second, letting the spawned fiber output its message. Another more natural way is to add Fiber.yield, which tells the scheduler to execute the other fiber(s).

Working with shared memory variables is a recipe for bugs. Instead, you'll want to let fibers pass values to each other through typed channels.

Channels and Shared Memory

 DO NOT COMMUNICATE BY SHARING MEMORY. That is, don't use shared variables to communicate data values!

Instead, *SHARE MEMORY BY COMMUNICATING.* That is, send/receive data values over channels.

What are these channels? They're objects of class Channel(T)—indeed, Channel is a generic class. They can pass typed values from one fiber to another. The following schema by Stanislav Kozlovski[3] illustrates concurrency in Crystal:

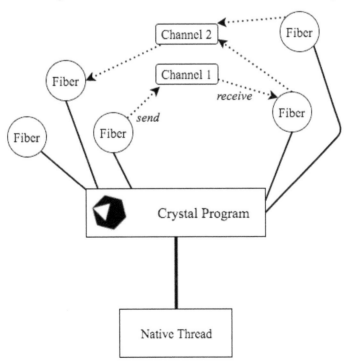

---

3.   https://hackernoon.com/crystal-the-ruby-youve-never-heard-of-57bad2efac9c

Synchronizing Data Flows

Not only are values sent over channels safe from data races, the sending and receiving of the values allows for a natural method of synchronization. Internally, a channel implements all the locking mechanisms needed to avoid data races. Take a look at this example—you'll see that main sends a value 42 over a channel to be received by the fiber. What will the output be?

```
advanced_features/main_fiber2.cr
ch = Channel(Int32).new

spawn do
  puts "start fiber"
  n = ch.receive # fiber will block here if nothing on the channel yet
  puts "fiber received #{n}"
end

puts "before send"
ch.send 42
puts "main has send 42"

# =>
```
❶ before send
❷ start fiber
❸ fiber received 42
❹ main has send 42

Look at the output of the program:

First comes line ❶ because the fiber hasn't started yet. Then main sends a value, and it's blocked until a value is received. This means the fiber can start in line ❷, receiving the value in line ❸, and then ends. Now main can continue and line ❹ is printed. In the same way, a fiber (or main) that receives on a channel is blocked until a value is sent on that channel. Sending a value immediately switches to the fiber waiting on that channel to receive, and then execution continues on that fiber.

Sending and receiving values, even the value nil, naturally synchronizes the execution of fibers.

Your Turn 2

➤ a. main_fiber3: Now let the fiber send the value and main receive it. Explain the output.

➤ b. main_fiber4: Let main send the numbers 1 to 10 over a channel while a fiber prints them out. Then again reverse the receiving and sending.

Waiting with the Event Loop

In the following code snippet, you can see the event loop in action: the fiber waits for input from the keyboard, and main waits to receive a value:

```
advanced_features/main_fiber5.cr
ch = Channel(String).new
spawn do
  while line = gets
    ch.send(line)
  end
end

puts ch.receive

# For example:
# =>
# hello
# hello
```

(Compile and execute this example on the command line.)

This is the case for any I/O, like receiving values over a network socket, or reading from a file.

Fiber Executing a Method

In many cases, a fiber will be given a method to execute with argument values, so it's created in a one-liner like this: spawn method1 argumentlist. In fact, here spawn is used as a macro. Take a look at the following example:

```
advanced_features/spawn_method.cr
def pname(name)
  3.times do |i|
    puts "#{name} - #{i}"
  end
end

spawn pname "spawned" # started on another fiber (in background)
pname("normal")       # started by main fiber
Fiber.yield
# =>
# normal - 0
# normal - 1
# normal - 2
# spawned - 0
# spawned - 1
# spawned - 2
```

The method pname is first called in a fiber and then through main.

Signaling the End of Execution

Here's another example—it shows how a worker fiber signals the end of its
execution by sending a value over a channel, which main then receives:

advanced_features/synchronizing.cr

```
# # Synchronization of channels:
# background worker signals on channel when it is done
# main fiber only continues when that signal is received
def worker(done : Channel(Bool))
  puts "worker: working"
  sleep 2
  puts "worker: done"
  done.send true
end

done = Channel(Bool).new
spawn worker(done)

done.receive # main blocks here
puts "main: next"

# =>
# worker: working
# worker: done
# main: next
```

Buffered Channels

The channels we've used until now can contain only one value. That's why
the switch from the sending to the receiving fiber happens instantly. But we
also have *buffered channels* that can contain a certain number of values,
specified when the channel is initialized:

advanced_features/buffered_channel.cr

```
ch = Channel(Char).new(2) # A buffered channel of capacity 2

spawn do
  puts "Before send 1"
  ch.send('\u03B1')
  puts "Before send 2"
  ch.send('\u03B2')
  if ch.empty?
    puts "Channel is empty"
  else
    puts "Channel is not empty"
  end
  puts "Before send 3"
  ch.send('\u03C9')
  puts "After send"
end
```

```
3.times do |i|
  puts ch.receive
end

# =>
# Before send 1
# Before send 2
# Channel is not empty
# Before send 3
# α
# β
# After send
# ω
```

Here, the switch to another fiber will occur only when the buffer is full. That's why α and β are printed one after the other. You can test whether a channel still contains a value with the empty? method. You can close a channel when you're finished with it and then test it with the closed? method.

Selecting a Fiber

Suppose several fibers are working concurrently and you want to do something as soon as any one of them returns a result. Crystal has a select when statement that does just that:

advanced_features/channel_select.cr
```
def generator(n : T) forall T
  chan = Channel(T).new
  spawn do
    loop do
      sleep n
      chan.send n
    end
  end
  chan
end

ch1 = generator(1)
ch2 = generator(1.5)
ch3 = generator(5)

loop do
  select
  when n1 = ch1.receive
    puts "Int: #{n1}"
  when f1 = ch2.receive
    puts "Float: #{f1}"
  when ch3.receive
    break
  end
end
```

```
# Output:
# Int: 1
# Float: 1.5
# Int: 1
# Float: 1.5
# Int: 1
# Int: 1
# Float: 1.5
```

Here, three fibers are created, each with its own channel. Each fiber has to sleep for a number of seconds (its argument), and then sends that argument on the channel. It repeats these actions in an infinite loop. Because the seconds argument is given as an integer and as a float, we write a generic method generator. Notice you have to add the keyword forall T to declare a method as generic.

main then receives the values from the channels in an infinite loop through select when. The loop is stopped with break after five seconds when channel ch3 returns a value.

Working with Files

The last example also teaches you how to work with files in the context of fibers. Can you figure out what the following code does before executing it?

advanced_features/lines_files.cr
```
ch = Channel(Int32).new
total_lines = 0
files = Dir.glob("*.txt")

files.each do |f|
  spawn do
    lines = File.read_lines(f).size
    ch.send lines
  end
end

files.size.times do
  total_lines += ch.receive
end

puts "Total number of lines in text files: #{total_lines}"
# => Total number of lines in text files: 7
```

You probably guessed it: the Dir.glob method accepts a pattern and returns an Array with all of the file names that correspond to that pattern—here, the .txt files. Then, a fiber is spawned for each text file that reads the file's lines into an Array, whose size is the number of lines. At the end, the fiber sends this result over the channel. The main thread loops over the number of files, receiving the line-count for each of them and summing them all up.

This is a common idiom in concurrent programming:

- Determine the number of separate tasks.
- Spawn a fiber for each task.
- Let main aggregate and report the results.

Let's now turn to another important aspect of many applications: databases.

Accessing Databases

Crystal can work with a growing number[4] of SQL and NoSQL databases. Among them are SQLite, MySQL (or MariaDB), Postgres, MongoDB,[5] Redis,[6] and ReThinkDB.[7]

The Crystal team realized the importance of database access for a programming language, so they made a DB module in a package called crystal-db,[8] which provides a common unified database API. Crystal-db works seamlessly together with the SQLite, MySQL, and Postgres driver. You don't need to explicitly require it. For other databases, you will need to add specific drivers.

Let's illustrate the basic database operations using the SQLite sample database chinook.db. This database represents a music shop and contains tables artists and albums among others. Because of crystal-db, how the operations are written is essentially the same for other databases.

First create a Crystal project (name it crchinook) with the command $ crystal init app crchinook. Then you need to add the shard crystal-sqlite3 by editing your shard.yml file with:

```
dependencies:
  sqlite3:
    github: crystal-lang/crystal-sqlite3
```

Next, issue the $ shards command to install this dependency. You'll write all the code in src/crchinook.cr. Don't forget to add require "sqlite3" at the top. In the following code snippet, you can see how common db actions are done:

advanced_features/crchinook/src/crchinook.cr
```
require "./crchinook/*"
require "sqlite3"

DB.open "sqlite3://../chinook.db" do |db|
```

---

4. https://github.com/veelenga/awesome-crystal#database-driversclients
5. https://github.com/datanoise/mongo.cr
6. https://github.com/stefanwille/crystal-redis
7. https://github.com/stefanwille/crystal-redis
8. https://github.com/crystal-lang/crystal-db

```
❶    sql = "SELECT artistid, name FROM artists ORDER BY name ASC;"
     db.query sql do |rs|
       p "#{rs.column_name(1)} (#{rs.column_name(0)})"
       rs.each do # perform for each row in the ResultSet
         artistid = rs.read(Int32)
         name = rs.read(String)
         p "#{name} (#{artistid})"
         # => Name (ArtistId)
         # => A Cor Do Som (43)
         # => AC/DC (1)
         # => Aaron Copland & London Symphony Orchestra (230)
         # => ...
       end
     end
❷    sql = "SELECT name FROM artists WHERE artistid = 231;"
     p db.query_one sql, as: String
     # => "Ton Koopman"
❸    sql = "SELECT MIN(birthdate) FROM employees;"
     oldest = db.scalar sql  # => "1947-09-19 00:00:00"
❹    sql = "SELECT firstname, lastname FROM employees WHERE birthdate = ?;"
     firstname, lastname = db.query_one sql, oldest, as: {String, String}
     p "#{firstname} #{lastname}"  # => "Margaret Park"
❺    db.exec "insert into artists values (?, ?)", 276, "Scott Ross"
     args = [] of DB::Any
     args << 277
     args << "Bernard Foccroules"
     db.exec "insert into artists values (?, ?)", args
❻    sql = "SELECT name FROM sqlite_master WHERE type='table';"
     db.query_all(sql, as: String)
     # =>
     # [ "albums",
     #   "sqlite_sequence",
     #   "artists",
     #   "customers",
     #   "employees",
     #   ...,
     #   "sqlite_stat1"
     # ]
end
```

❶ Read all artists.

❷ Read one artist by artistid.

❸ Read one value with scalar.

❹ Read oldest employee by substituting a variable.

❺ Use exec for DDL (Data Definition) statements.

❻ Read all table names.

Build the app with $ crystal build src/crchinook.cr and run it with $ ./crchinook.

Make a connection with the database by providing DB.open with a connection URI as the argument. These take the forms:

- sqlite3:///path/to/data.db
- mysql://user:password@server:port/database
- postgres://server:port/database

By using DB.open with a do end block, the database connection is automatically closed at end. If this isn't appropriate, you have to use the following pattern:

```
db = DB.open "sqlite3://../chinook.db"
begin
  # ... use db to perform queries
ensure
  db.close
end
```

db or DB.open creates a DB::Database object that automatically provides you with a *connection pool*—that is, several database connections are made available to execute your queries. This pool can be configured[9] for maximum number of connections, checkout time, retry number, and retry delay.

Getting the Database Type

You can extract the database type from the database URIs shown here with db.uri.scheme. This comes in handy when you need to tailor the SQL according to the database. Just use case...when, like shown here:

```
sql = case db.uri.scheme
      when "postgres"
        # SQL for postgres
      when "mysql"
        # SQL for mysql
      when "sqlite3"
        # SQL for sqlite3
      else
        raise "SQL not implemented for #{db.uri.scheme}"
      end
```

Select queries are done with the query method, which returns a ResultSet object. You can iterate over that object with the each method to obtain and process each row successively. You should indicate the type of each field, as in rs.read(Int32), because at compilation time there is no type information about specific database fields available. The minimum set of types supported is

---

9. https://crystal-lang.org/docs/database/connection_pool.html

given in DB::Types, and includes Nil, String, Bool, Int32, Int64, Float32, Float64, Time, and Bytes. The type DB::Any is an alias for any of them because it is the union of all these types.

The column names can be accessed by index as rs.column_name(1), or returned as an array with column_names. Multiple columns can be read at once like this: artistid, name = rs.read(Int32, String). Use query_one to read one row, scalar to read the first value of the first row, and query_all specified as: Type to return an array.

Queries ❹ and ❺ in the crchinook listing show how values can be interpolated into a SQL string by using one or more ? in the case of SQLite. For Postgres, you have to use $1 and $2. Each database has its own approach to this. Using parameters in your SQL statements like this avoids SQL injection.

For queries that create database objects or change values (insert, update, delete), use the exec method, as in line ❺. You see that for insert statements, you can just populate an array and substitute it in the ? value placeholders. Then in line ❻ we use query_all to read all table names from the database, so use it only if you don't mind getting all records back! query_all executes a query and returns an array where the first column's value of each row is read as the given type. Here[10] are the docs of all available query methods.

SQL statements that need to be executed together can also be enveloped in a transaction.

Exception Handling with Databases

 All interactions with a database can give exceptions for various reasons, so in production code you should envelop that code within a begin ... rescue ... ensure ... end block.

If you'd rather move a step up the abstraction ladder, you might want to use an ORM (Object-Relational Mapping) framework. Crystal offers many choices, which you can explore at awesome crystal[11] or crystalshards.[12] Good places to start include:

- topaz,[13] which is a simple DB wrapper.

- crecto,[14] inspired by the Ecto framework in Elixir to be used in larger projects. It even contains an admin dashboard.

---

10. http://crystal-lang.github.io/crystal-db/api/latest/DB/QueryMethods.html
11. https://github.com/veelenga/awesome-crystal#ormodm-extensions
12. https://crystalshards.org/?filter=orm
13. https://github.com/topaz-crystal/topaz
14. https://github.com/Crecto/crecto

- granite-orm,[15] which is used with the amber web framework, specifically for Postgres, MySQL, and SQLite.

You can find out much more about the many available DB objects and methods in the docs.[16]

A Company's Story Crystallized: NeuraLegion

Art Linkov and *Bar Hofesh* are the founders of NeuraLegion,[17] a new startup company based in Israel that has a passion to make the world a better place through machine learning and artificial intelligence (AI). They are currently focusing on the cyber security world.

Ivo: *What production projects do you use Crystal for?*

Bar Hofesh: *NexPloit is our first product using Crystal. It aims to redefine Software Penetration Testing through the power of AI and provides a fully automatic solution for detection of software vulnerabilities.*

Ivo: *Why did you decide to use Crystal for this application?*

Bar Hofesh: *When we started working on NexPloit, we were already long-time fans of Ruby. We love Ruby because it is object oriented by default, making it easy to use; it is versatile and has a good pool of libraries developed by the community. In addition, we find Ruby beautiful and well matured as a programming language.*

However, when we rolled up our sleeves and began to develop, there were some innate characteristics of Ruby that did not fulfill our needs. To name a few examples:

- *Ruby does not provide explicit types. This has several implications for performance, sizing penalties, and unnecessary manipulations the data has to go though. For our purposes, efficiency was a very important issue.*

- *To solve the previous problem, C bindings are often used. However, they can be very tricky to implement with Ruby. As we mentioned already, Ruby does not have explicit types. C, on the other hand, is a strongly typed language, but consciously knowing at any given time which type exactly to pass around can be a little daunting, and might take a few tries to make it work.*

- *undefined method for nil:NilClass. If you are someone who has worked with Ruby before, you won't need any explanations here. If not, you might recognize this error on other dynamic, non-compiled languages where you try to call on a method to something you thought would be an object, but in runtime became nil for some reason. The disadvantage is that when no checks are performed during compile time (or other stages of evaluations), you are left to debug the program fully in runtime.*

---

15. https://github.com/amberframework/granite-orm
16. http://crystal-lang.github.io/crystal-db/api/latest/
17. https://www.neuralegion.com/

- *When executing our programs written in Ruby, the performance was limited.*

For these reasons and some others, we needed a programming language that had all the advantages of Ruby, but without the disadvantages. That's when we discovered Crystal, and we almost immediately fell in love with it ❤.

Ivo: *How was your experience developing with Crystal?*

Bar Hofesh: *Crystal's slick coding experience, ease of lower-level library bindings, type safety in compile-time without the need to even execute the program, and finally the lightning-fast runtime performance gave us what we needed to really set the keyboard on fire! We can honestly say that Crystal gave us the tools to elegantly and efficiently take NexPloit and take it from an idea into a reality.*

Ivo: *What would you like to see improved in Crystal?*

Bar Hofesh: *We love Crystal, but there is always some room for improvement. One of the challenges we faced with Crystal was the lack of shards (Crystal's "gems") for machine learning and scientific tools. However, expecting other people to add shards is unfair, so we decided to create a shard for Crystal-FANN as the groundwork for our needs, and we made it available on our Github page[18] for anyone who may need it. For now, Crystal-FANN seems to hit the spot for us, but we are still considering the addition of Torch or TensorFlow if we conclude that FANN by itself is not enough.*

Wrapping Up

In this chapter, you learned to appreciate the power of macros, but also to be cautious in applying them. You saw how easy it is to bind to C programs from Crystal. We dug deeper into how Crystal executes as a cooperative factory of fibers. Using concurrency when appropriate can improve your performance for many kinds of projects. Last, you saw how you can easily integrate your app with a wide range of databases.

In the next (and final) chapter, you'll see what Crystal has to offer in the realm of web frameworks. We'll conclude with a discussion of the most important shards in various application areas.

---

18. https://github.com/NeuraLegion/crystal-fann

## CHAPTER 9

Using Web Frameworks and Shards

So far, you've been learning about the details of the Crystal language. There's much more to Crystal than the language specifications, with a wide variety of libraries and frameworks available to help you out.

This chapter will give you a foundation for building your own web apps in Crystal using Kemal. We'll also take you on a brief tour of the constantly growing and evolving shard ecosystem, pointing out some important shards that can help make your Crystal apps more successful. You don't need to do all the work yourself!

Build Web Applications with the Kemal and Amber Frameworks

Ruby's most explosive growth came from Rails, the outstanding web framework. As Crystal is a direct descendant of Ruby, it's not surprising that developers have poured energy into Crystal web frameworks. If you read through the company testimonies, you'll see that many of them use Kemal.

The Built-in Web Server

Crystal's standard library has a module HTTP for basic web techniques such as static file handling, logging, error-handling, form data, websockets, and so on. It also contains a built-in web server, the class HTTP::Server. You can set that up in just a few lines of code, and see the foundations of a running web server:

web_frameworks_and_shards/web_server.cr
```
require "http/server"

❶ server = HTTP::Server.new do |ctx|
❷   ctx.response.content_type = "text/plain"
❸   ctx.response.print "Crystal web server: got #{ctx.request.path}"
end
```

```
server.bind_tcp 8080
server.listen
puts "Crystal web server listening on http://localhost:8080"

# => in browser with the URL http://localhost:8080/
# "Crystal web server: got /"
```

To start using it, we need to require the HTTP module's code. Then, create an instance of the Server class in line ❶. A fiber spawns to handle each incoming request, so the Crystal web server is fully concurrent. The fiber will be given the code in the do end block to execute. It has access to a ctx parameter (an object of class Context), which contains info from the request, like its path: the address the client requested. Together with the block, a list of HTTP handlers can be processed (see the docs[1]).

In reply to the request, the processing fiber will set up the response of the server by specifying its content-type in line ❷. Because this is a minimalist reply, it's just text/plain. At this stage you could also set the status and header properties. Afterwards it will write (with print) to the response in line ❸. The server will send that to the web client (probably a browser), which will process the content and show it.

The server itself is bound to an IP address and port using the bind_tcp methods, and then started with the listen method in line ❹. If you add true to the end of the +argument list for bind_tcp, the web server will enable port reuse. This means that multiple sockets are allowed to bind to the same port on the same host, simulating multi-threaded behavior.

To parameterize the server's address as well as the port, you can bind the server like this:

```
ip = "0.0.0.0"
port = 8080
server.bind_tcp ip, port # ...
```

Compile this script with $ crystal web_server.cr. You'll see the message

```
Crystal web server listening on http://localhost:8080
```

appearing on the server console. Opening up a browser with this address will show you the server's response:

```
Crystal web server: got /
```

Stop the server with CTRL+C or use close in the code.

---

1. https://crystal-lang.org/api/latest/HTTP.html

This default web server has very good performance, but because you have to provide the basic building blocks yourself, you'll have to write a lot more code. An example of this is routing specific requests to their appropriate response. You may want to add tools to deal with this. router_cr[2] is a good minimal middleware for a Crystal web server.

The next sections visit other frameworks that are built on top of the basic http-server. Comparison benchmarks show that Crystal web frameworks are among the fastest, if not number one (see *Speeding Up the Web*, on page 9).

Your Turn 1

➤ a. An XML Time Server: Create a web server on port 5000 that shows the time and a greeting according to the time of day. Use XML as the output format. (Hint: Use "text/xml" as the content-type.)

➤ b. Serving an Index Page: Create a web server that does error-handling and logging, and serves an index.html page when the browser requests the URL http://127.0.0.1:3000/public. (Hints: Use the docs for the Handlers, and copy the page to output with IO.copy.)

Kemal: A Lightweight Web Framework

Kemal[3] is the lightning-fast defacto standard web framework for Crystal, developed by Serdar Dogruyol. It's the successor to Frank, a proof-of-concept framework written by the Crystal team. Kemal has a modular architecture. Most of its idioms come from Sinatra (a lightweight Ruby web framework), which is why simplicity is one of its hallmarks. Its CPU and memory requirements (+- 1MB) are very low: one server can handle tens of thousands of clients.

A Basic Kemal App

To start, let's build the example from Chapter 1, *Speeding Up the Web*, on page 9 from scratch.

You know the drill by now:

- Create a new app with crystal init (call it simple_kemal_app).

- Add the following section to the shard.yml file:

```
dependencies:
  kemal:
    github: kemalcr/kemal
```

- Issue the shards command.

- The output shows that in addition to kemal, two other dependent shards (radix, used for routing, and kilt, used for view templating) are also installed:

```
Installing kemal
Installing radix (0.3.8)
Installing kilt (0.4.0)
```

Remember: This step installs the source code of Kemal in the /lib folder, and it is pure Crystal, so you can see for yourself how it all works!

Now add the following code into src/simple_kemal_app.cr:

web_frameworks_and_shards/simple_kemal_app/src/simple_kemal_app.cr
```
require "./simple_kemal_app/*"
```
❶
```
require "kemal"
```
❷
```
get "/" do
  "My first Kemal app is alive!"
end
```
❸
```
Kemal.run
```

Then run the app with crystal src/simple_kemal_app.cr (or use crystal build and run the executable). The following message will appear:

```
[development] Kemal is ready to lead at http://0.0.0.0:3000
```

Open up a browser with the address http://localhost:3000/ (the default port is 3000) and you'll see the message: "My first Kemal app is alive!"

Meanwhile, on the Kemal console you see something like this:

```
2017-10-04 10:10:17 +0200 200 GET / 165.0µs
2017-10-04 10:10:17 +0200 404 GET /favicon.ico 204.0µs
...
^CKemal is going to take a rest!
```

This default output logging can be disabled by setting logging false. You can also define your own custom logging if wanted. Or, to change the default port, for example to 8080, use the code Kemal.config.port = 8080.

The code for responding to requests is elegant and simple:

❶ require the Kemal shard.

❷ Match a GET "http://localhost:3000/" request by returning an output string to the client.

❸ Start the web server by calling the run method.

If you would prefer to tell the browser to visit an index page to answer this request, you can do it like this:

```
get "/" do |env|
  env.redirect "index.html"
end
```

env is the environment variable and must be given as a parameter to the handler block, so get "/" do must change to get "/" do |env|. env is useful because it can access all info about the request and parameters (received through the URL, query, or as posted form parameter), and it can configure and fill in the response. It has also set and get methods to store a value during the request/response cycle.

Kemal can handle all HTTP methods such as GET, POST, PUT, PATCH, and DELETE: the routing handler is always a do end code block, which can have a context variable. This provides your app with a RESTful web service architecture. Routes are handled in the order they are defined: the first route that matches the request URL will be activated.

Using Views with ECR

Let's start building a simple website, exploring more of Kemal's features along the way. To show dynamic pages constructed partly through code, Kemal can use the ECR (Embedded Crystal)[4] module.

This is a template language from the standard library used for embedding Crystal code into text like HTML, much as ERB does in Ruby. Unlike ERB, however, all templates are compiled into just one string, which is pretty efficient: you suffer no performance penalty when doing heavy templating. ECR templates are also type-safe.

But enough theory—let's get started. First create a project called appviews. To ease development you can use the *sentry*[5] command-line interface tool, written for Crystal by Samuel Eaton. This watches your source files, and it will build and run the app automatically when it detects a change in them. That way, you don't have to stop and restart an app on every change! Install it within the app folder with:

```
$ curl -fsSLo- https://raw.githubusercontent.com/samueleaton/sentry/master/install.cr | crystal eval
```

(Notice how this uses crystal eval, evaluating the script install.cr.)

---

4.   https://crystal-lang.org/api/latest/ECR.html
5.   https://github.com/samueleaton/sentry

To execute this tool, do $ ./sentry. It starts watching:

```
ivo@ivo-SATELLITE-L50D-B:~/crystal/Book/code/web_frameworks_and_shards/appviews$ ./sentry
🐾 Your SentryBot is vigilant. beep-boop...
🐾 watching file: ./src/appviews/version.cr
🐾 watching file: ./src/appviews.cr
🐾 compiling appviews...
🐾 starting appviews...
```

Add the following to .gitignore to remove sentry and the executables from source control:

```
/doc/
/lib/
/bin/
/.shards/
/dev/
sentry
appviews
```

Then follow the steps from the previous section to install Kemal. Also write its code inside src/appviews.cr: because sentry is at work, it will see this, compile your app, and start running Kemal!

Now we probably want to add some static files, like JavaScripts and stylesheets. We'll use Bootstrap here (use the minified version for a production app) and our app's stylesheet in appviews.css. All these assets are placed in a public folder like this:

```
appviews/
  src/
    appviews.cr
  public/
    images/
    fonts/
    js/
      bootstrap.js
      appviews.js
    css/
      bootstrap.css
      appviews.css
    index.html
```

Kemal will find assets in the public folder automatically, pointing to them with paths like /js/appviews.js. If you have no static files, you can disable this by setting serve_static false in your code. Or you can change the location as well, like this: public_folder "src/public". We won't use an index.html in this example.

Instead of a simple greeting, it's time to show a home page using ECR. We can do this by changing the get handler in src/appviews.cr to:

```
get "/" do
  title = "Home"
  page_message = "Your app's home page"
  render "src/views/home.ecr"
end
```

This introduces two variables, title and page_message. For the first time, we see how ECR is used: you render an .ecr template, which is placed in src/views, the location for these template files or *views*. Before trying that out, you need an ECR file. Edit a new file, home.ecr, in that folder, adding this content:

```
<div class="jumbotron">
  <h2><%= page_message %></h2>
  <p>Your home page text starts here ...</p>
  <p><a class="btn btn-lg btn-primary" href="#" role="button">Learn
  more &raquo;</a></p>
</div>
```

Now sentry compiles and your browser shows this at http://localhost:3000:

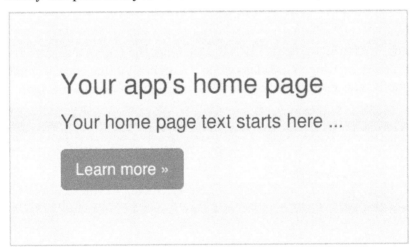

What has happened here? In <%= page_message %> the value of page_message was pasted in the home view, which is what <%= %> does. You can also put Crystal code inside <% %> to control execution.

For common navigation, header, footer code, and so on, you can use a layout or several. These are also .ecr pages that you put in a subfolder of views called layouts. Create a main_layout.cr in that folder. It's mainly a lot of HTML, which we aren't going to show here (but it's in the sample code file).

This layout will be used if you replace the previous render line with the following:

```
render "src/views/home.ecr", "src/views/layouts/main_layout.ecr"
```

How does it work? The layout page sets the web page title via <%= title %>. It also contains this section:

```
<div class="container">
    <%= content %>
</div>
```

home.ecr is shown within the layout page because, in Kemal, the variable content captures the content of the first argument to render. Depending on the view, you might need different JavaScript or other chunks of HTML or stylesheets. In that case, content_for and yield_content come in handy; see the Kemal guide[6] for more detail.

We also see a code section, which sits in the <div> navbar:

```
<li <% if env.request.path == "/" %>class="active"<% end %>>
<a href="/">Home</a></li>
<li <% if env.request.path == "/about" %>class="active"<% end %>>
<a href="/about">About</a></li>
<li <% if env.request.path == "/contact" %>class="active"<% end %>>
<a href="/about">Contact</a></li>
```

This code, <% if [condition] %>[effect]<% end %>, tests the requested path through the env variable, setting a CSS class when it matches. At this stage, compilation will again be successful, and our website starts to have some design:

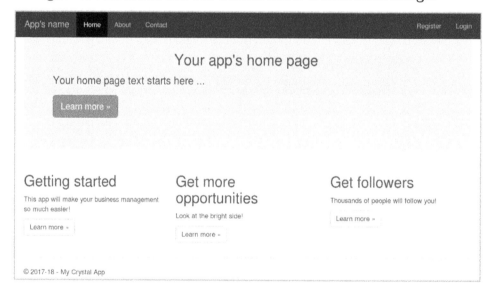

---

6.   http://kemalcr.com/guide/

Add the about.ecr and contact.ecr pages to the views folder, and add two get routing handlers to appviews.cr. Our two new pages will inherit the same look:

```
get "/about" do |env|
  title = "About"
  page_message = "Your app's description page"
  render "src/views/about.ecr", "src/views/layouts/main_layout.ecr"
end
get "/contact" do |env|
  title = "Contact"
  page_message = "Your app's contact page"
  render "src/views/contact.ecr", "src/views/layouts/main_layout.ecr"
end
```

Click on Register or Login, and Kemal will point out to you that these views don't yet exist. Play around to start building your own Kemal website!

Streaming Database Data with JSON

Sometimes you just want to send data, not HTML pages. Let's stream database data from the server to the client in JSON format, an example inspired by a blog article[7] from Brian Cardiff. We'll combine what we have learned in *Accessing Databases*, on page 167 about accessing databases and work with the same sqlite3 database, chinook.db. You can do the preliminary work by yourself: create an app called db_json and add the shards kemal and sqlite3.

The app's logic structure looks like this:

- Open a database connection.

- Define the GET route handlers:

    1) A root request / will return a list of the names of all tables.

    2) A request like /:table_name, for example /artists, will return all records in JSON format.

- Start the Kemal web server.

- Close the db connection.

The first handler is extremely concise. First, set the type of the server's response with env.response.content_type. Then, get the data. Execute the SQL query with query_all. Its result is an array, so you can use the to_json method on it. This creates a string with the JSON representation and sends it to the client. That's it!

---

7. https://manas.tech/blog/2017/01/16/from-a-db-to-json-with-crystal.html

```
get "/" do |env|
  env.response.content_type = "application/json"
  tables = table_names(db)
  tables.to_json
end

def table_names(db)
  sql = "SELECT name FROM sqlite_master WHERE type='table';"
  db.query_all(sql, as: String)
end
```

And here is the resulting output:

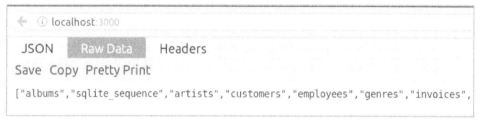

If you would rather see these table names in an HTML-based view, change the handler to:

```
get "/" do |env|
  tables = table_names(db)
  render "src/views/tables.ecr"
end
```

and add a view, tables.ecr, which loops over the tables array like this:

```
<header>
  <h1>All tables</h1>
</header>
<body>
    <% if tables %>
        <% tables.each do |table| %>
            <p><%= table %></p>
        <% end %>
    <% end %>
</body>
```

As shown in the figure on page 183 variables from the script (such as tables) are automatically known in the view!

The second handler is slightly more complicated. The table name is given as a parameter in the URL. This can be read through env.params.url as in line ❶ in the following code. To avoid SQL injection attacks, we check in line ❷ that the parameter is an existing table. We execute the query in line ❸ and loop over each record in line ❹, sending a JSON string to the client in the method write_json.

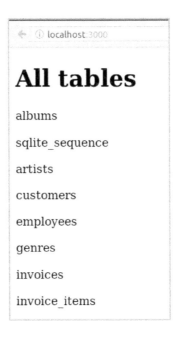

web_frameworks_and_shards/db_json/src/db_json.cr
```
get "/:table_name" do |env|
  env.response.content_type = "application/json"
  table_name = env.params.url["table_name"]
  # avoid SQL injection by checking table name
  unless table_names(db).includes?(table_name)
    # ignore if the requested table does not exist.
    env.response.status_code = 404
  else
    db.query "select * from #{table_name}" do |rs|
      col_names = rs.column_names
      rs.each do
        write_json(env.response.output, col_names, rs)
        # force chunked response even on small tables
        env.response.output.flush
      end
    end
  end
end
```

The mechanism used here is to stream one row at a time, minimizing memory usage on the server. The client will be able to process the data as it comes through. This is done by applying the flush method to the output buffer in line ❻, sending the JSON string immediately to the client, sometimes called a *chunked response*. The JSON string is constructed in the write_json method, which is called for each record:

web_frameworks_and_shards/db_json/src/db_json.cr

```
   def write_json(io, col_names, rs)
❶    JSON.build(io) do |json|
       json.object do
         col_names.each do |col|
❷          json_encode_field json, col, rs.read
         end
       end
     end
     io << "\n"
   end
```

The transformation of a ResultSet with column names and field values to JSON is a little more involved, so we'll need to use the JSON[8] module here.

Crystal-db is designed for speed and provides direct access to the database values in memory without the need to create temporary arrays or hashes. (If you create a lot of your own temporary arrays or hashes, of course, that may not help.) We create a JSON::Builder object in line ❶ in the preceding code that writes directly to io, which is the web server's output passed in line ❺.

To make it concrete, here is the JSON output of the first record of table artists: {"ArtistId":1,"Name":"AC/DC"}. json.object starts and ends the JSON string for one record and invokes the do code block. For each column, the name col is written, together with the value rs.read. This is done in json_encode_field in line ❷ below:

web_frameworks_and_shards/db_json/src/db_json.cr

```
   def json_encode_field(json, col, value)
     case value
❶    when Bytes
       json.field col do
         json.array do # writes begin and end of an array
           value.each do |e|
             json.scalar e # writes the value
           end
         end
       end
     else
       json.field col do      # write an object's field and value
❷        value.to_json(json)
       end
     end
   end
```

This invokes the method to_json on all simple database values in line ❷, but for the Bytes type in line ❶ we need to be more careful, treating it as an array

---

8. https://crystal-lang.org/api/latest/JSON.html

and looping over each value. This way does not create a temporary array, so it is the most efficient way to process objects that could be big blobs.

You can find the source code as a whole in the download code db_json/src/db_json.cr. Here you see the output of the first ten rows from the table artists:

Other Features and Example Web Apps

Based on the example code we've discussed so far, you should be able to combine ECR views with database data to build more real-world database web apps. But there's a lot more you can do with Crystal and Kemal. Here are some other Kemal examples that might inspire you:

- A todo app[9] demo, developed with Kemal, React, and PostgreSQL using websockets.

- A chat app[10] demo here.[11]

- An app[12] using JWT authentication with auth0 described in detail here.[13]

- A blog app.[14]

- A blog server called kamber.[15]

- Kemal-watcher[16] is a plugin-like sentry plugin that watches client files.

- See how you can easily send SMS messages[17] or make telephone calls[18] by using the Twilio API.

9.   https://github.com/Angarsk8/realtime-todo-app
10. https://github.com/Angarsk8/chat-app-demo
11. http://kemal-react-chat.herokuapp.com/
12. https://github.com/rbnpercy/challenge
13. https://auth0.com/blog/building-your-first-crystal-app-with-jwt-authentication/
14. https://github.com/sdogruyol/kemal-blog
15. https://github.com/f/kamber
16. https://github.com/faustinoaq/kemal-watcher
17. https://www.twilio.com/blog/2016/11/send-sms-messages-crystal.html
18. https://www.twilio.com/blog/2016/12/make-phone-calls-crystal-twilio.html

These few examples give just a taste of Kemal's strengths. For inspiration, here are more possibilities you should explore:

- Request *parameters* are easy to work with—for example, if the request is /users/108, then the handler get "/users/:id" matches this, and the value 108 is retrieved through env.params.url["id"].

- You can insert *filters* in the response cycle that let you create and encapsulate your own logic, manipulating the request or response. They come as before_x or after_x, where x can be: get, post, put, patch, delete or all.

- Kemal's modularity is achieved through *handlers* (or *middlewares*) similar to Rack middleware: these are classes that inherit from Kemal::Handler, and can be called conditionally based on the request method. Built-in are logging, exception, static-file, and route handling. Other middlewares for basic authentication and csrf protection are available.

- Kemal can store info in *sessions* by including the kemal-session[19] shard. The data can be stored in memory, file, Redis, and even MySQL.

- Kemal has easy *websocket* support (see the chat app, for example), which works much faster than Node.js. (Though really, this power comes from the built-in web server.)

- You can test your web app by using the spec-kemal shard.

- Kemal gives you access to cookies, file uploads, built-in SSL support, ability to differentiate between test and production environments, custom error handling, email-sending via smtp.cr,[20] and multi-DB support.

- You can deploy your app on Heroku or through a Capistrano script.

Kemal's[21] website does an excellent job showing how to use the many different features of this framework. Raze[22] is a younger framework that aims to compete with Kemal.

Amber: A Rails-Like Web Framework

Kemal is a fast and fully featured web server, but it's deliberately minimal. If you'd like to have a framework do more for you, offering services like Ruby on Rails, Crystal offers a few Rails-like frameworks. Unsurprisingly, they rely heavily on macros internally.

---

19. https://github.com/kemalcr/kemal-session
20. https://github.com/raydf/smtp.cr
21. http://kemalcr.com/guide/
22. https://razecr.com/

Amber[23] is inspired by Kemal, Rails, Phoenix, and other popular application frameworks, and it follows the MVC (Model-View-Controller) pattern. You can find its source code here,[24] where you can see that it's growing at a fast pace. They also have joined forces with Kemalyst,[25] which is also based on Kemal.

The Amber developers aim to build a Rails for Crystal. Amber uses the conventions of a typical MVC framework, providing code generation and scaffolding for quick prototype construction. By default, it uses the lightweight granite[26] ORM (Object Relational Mapper) for working with databases using minimal configuration, providing you with easy queries such as find_by and all, and one-to-many relations belong_to and has_many. But you can also opt for the Crecto (like Phoenix ecto) or (more full featured) Jennifer ORMs.

Amber uses a built-in command-line tool called amber. It can generate a project skeleton for you, complete with models, controllers, and views. Route handling is done with pipes, as in Phoenix.

By default, applications are configured to use a PostgreSQL database adapter, but this can be switched to MySQL, SQLite, or any other datastore or microservice you need to use. The default rendering engine is Slang, but ECR can be used as well. Amber builds in Sentry for smooth development. In addition to handling HTTP requests, Amber apps can work with websockets and can do mailing out-of-the-box.

If all this makes you want to get started right away with Amber, start here.[27]

There are some other frameworks in this area worth mentioning, such as Amethyst,[28] carbon-crystal,[29] and Lucky[30] by the Thoughtbot company. For a websocket-first framework, look at lattice-core.[31]

A Brief Tour of the Shard Ecosystem

The Crystal ecosystem is growing rapidly: at the time of writing, more than 3700 shards are available in very diverse fields. Let's first list the places where you should go "hunting" for shards:

---

23. https://amberframework.org/
24. https://github.com/amberframework/amber
25. https://github.com/kemalyst/kemalyst
26. https://github.com/amberframework/granite-orm
27. https://amberframework.org/guides
28. http://codcore.github.io/amethyst/
29. https://github.com/benoist/carbon-crystal
30. http://luckyframework.org/
31. https://github.com/jasonl99/lattice-core

- Your first stop should be Libhunt,[32] which is a curated list sorted into more than 50 categories.

- Another curated list is Awesome Crystal.[33]

- Crystal Shards[34] is a simple find mechanism, which also shows the trending, most popular, and recently updated projects.

- Crystal ANN[35] is THE place where new projects, versions, blogs, or anything new to Crystal is announced.

It's nearly impossible to even list, let alone discuss, the most useful shards. Concerning the web and databases, we already linked to a lot of important shards in this and the previous chapter. Here are some useful shards that are worth studying, some of which show the DSL-like capabilities of Crystal.

Job Processing

- Sidekiq[36] is a simple and efficient background job processing framework that is four times faster than its API-compatible Ruby predecessor.[37] Sidekiq uses Kemal to render all dashboards and web UI in the app.

- Schedule[38] and cron_scheduler[39] are useful for implementing job scheduling.

Deployment

- Baked File System[40] allows you to store all your static files into a single binary to facilitate deployment.

Graphics and GUI

- Most promising is Qt5.cr,[41] which provides bindings to the Qt5 framework, and libui,[42] which provides bindings to the native C GUI library for Linux, OS X, and Windows. crystal-gl[43] is an Open-GL binding in the works.

---

32. https://crystal.libhunt.com/categories
33. http://awesomelists.top/#/repos/veelenga/awesome-crystal
34. http://crystalshards.org/
35. https://crystal-ann.com/
36. https://github.com/mperham/sidekiq.cr
37. http://sidekiq.org
38. https://github.com/hugoabonizio/schedule.cr
39. https://github.com/kostya/cron_scheduler
40. https://github.com/schovi/baked_file_system
41. https://github.com/Papierkorb/qt5.cr
42. https://github.com/Fusion/libui.cr
43. https://github.com/ggiraldez/crystal-gl

Games

- For developing video games and multimedia applications, use CrSFML.[44] Cray[45] provides complete bindings to the extremely simple RayLib C library with audio, 2D, 3D, shaders, keyboard/mouse/gamepad/touch input, image manipulation, and more. Glove[46] is another framework that is in full development.

Artificial Intelligence and Machine Learning

- Crystal-fann[47] is a Fast Artificial Neural Network binding in Crystal, developed by the company NeuraLegion for its products.

- Ai4cr[48] is a port of the Ruby Playground for AI researchers.

Tooling

- crystal-futures[49] is an implementation of futures as you would see in JavaScript.

- Crystal-clear[50] implements Design by Contract using macros.

Bindings to Third-Party APIs

- Twitter-crystal[51] is a library to access the Twitter API.
- There are bindings for the Salesforce REST API, as well as for Spotify, Google Maps, Docker, GitHub, Slack, SoundCloud, and many others.

A Company's Story Crystallized: Kemal in Production

Kemal is deployed in production apps by the following companies, including:

- Protel:[52] This is a fortune 500 company that builds POS (Point Of Sales) systems. It has used Kemal, for example, to process payment requests, and discovered that 100 Unicorn (Ruby) workers could be replaced by a single Kemal process.

---

44. https://github.com/oprypin/crsfml
45. https://gitlab.com/Zatherz/cray
46. https://github.com/ddfreyne/glove
47. https://github.com/NeuraLegion/crystal-fann
48. https://github.com/drhuffman12/ai4cr
49. https://github.com/dhruvrajvanshi/crystal-futures
50. https://github.com/Groogy/crystal-clear
51. https://github.com/sferik/twitter-crystal
52. https://www.protel.com.tr/en

- Rainforest:[53] This company specializes in QA testing for web and mobile apps, and exploratory testing. It uses Kemal for microservices.
- Bulutfon:[54] This company offers VOIP solutions in Turkey. It also had scaling problems with Ruby, which were solved by changing to Kemal.

Kemal is somewhat different from other approaches. For static file service, Kemal is fast enough that there is no need to use Nginx for that. However, if Kemal's lack of multithreading worries you, put Nginx in front of Kemal in a reverse proxy setup, as they work well together. Port reuse might also be a simple answer. The Kemal app server doesn't handle process management, supervision, and monitoring, so use specialized apps such as Monit or init.d, or runit for process supervision.

Wrapping Up and Afterword

In this chapter, we looked at the strength of Crystal in the web world: its built-in fast http-server, the lightweight and blazingly fast Kemal web framework, and lastly, the full-fledged Amber web framework. You also got the keys to the treasure chest of Crystal shards.

This brings us to the end of our Crystal journey in this book. We hope you've enjoyed it as much as we enjoyed writing it. We hope that this whirlwind overview has shown you why Crystal is a rising star in the software development world, and why you'll want to use Crystal in your projects. Join the Crystal community[55] and apply your coding talents. Perhaps we'll meet again in the Crystal universe.

---

53. https://www.rainforestqa.com
54. https://www.bulutfon.com
55. https://crystal-lang.org/community/

Part IV

Appendices

Here you'll see how to set up Crystal, find a quick guide to help you convert Ruby code to Crystal, and answers to the questions in the "Your Turn" sections.

Setting Up a Crystal Environment

In this chapter, you'll get up and running with Crystal, and by the end of it, you'll write, compile, and execute your first code in a Crystal-friendly environment. You'll begin by installing the Crystal compiler and tool-chain. Then we'll discuss the compilation process and editor options so that you can write your source code comfortably. Next, you'll learn to work with the Crystal Playground: this is like a modern graphical version of a REPL (a Read Execute Print Loop, such as irb or pry for Ruby).

Working with Crystal Online

If you'd like to take Crystal for a test drive before installing it, you can use the online version of Crystal playground[1] for your preferred browser. This is effectively a sandbox in the cloud—a web service that compiles your code, runs it, and displays the result. It provides an edit screen with a "Compile & run code" button:

---

1.   https://play.crystal-lang.org

This takes you to an output screen. From here, you can save the source in a local file:

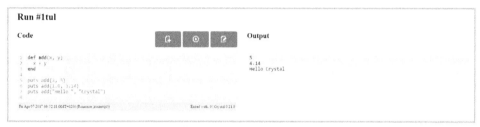

Tio[2] offers another fun way to run Crystal online.

Installing Crystal on Your Machine

You can find detailed installation instructions and remarks for the various Linux distros, OS X, and Windows on this page.[3]

The easiest way to get up and running with a stable version is to download the binary installer[4] for your platform. Simply unzip it and add the folder with the binary executable (e.g., /usr/bin/crystal on Linux) to your path.

Installing Crystal for Mac OS X users is a breeze, thanks to Homebrew.

$ brew update

$ brew install crystal

To update to a newer version, you do the following:

$ brew update

$ brew upgrade crystal-lang

Now let's follow the steps for a Debian/Ubuntu installation, which uses the official Crystal repository. (The procedure is very similar for other Linux-based systems.) Debian doesn't (yet) know about Crystal by default, so first, add the repository to your software installer:

$ curl https://dist.crystal-lang.org/apt/setup.sh | sudo bash

If you have concerns about the security of this command, you can instead execute the following commands as root:

---

2. https://tio.run/#crystal

3. https://crystal-lang.org/docs/installation/

4. https://github.com/crystal-lang/crystal/releases

```
$ curl -sL "https://keybase.io/crystal/pgp_keys.asc" | sudo apt-key add -
```

```
$ echo "deb https://dist.crystal-lang.org/apt crystal main" | sudo tee /etc/apt/sources.list.d/crystal.list
```

```
$ apt-get update
```

Install the stable Crystal version with:

```
$ sudo apt install crystal
```

That's all there is to it! Upgrading to a newer version will probably happen when you update your system generally. If not, do the following:

```
$ sudo apt-get update
```

and repeat the install step.

Note that at the time of this writing, the complete Windows port is a work in progress. For now, you can run Crystal only on Windows 10 through Bash, so you have to install the Linux subsystem and run your Crystal program in it. Here[5] is an easy way to get started. (You might want to install the Linux libraries mentioned here.[6] They are needed to run the Crystal Playground.)

If you really want to get into examining Crystal and contributing, clone the source code[7] and compile it with a previous Crystal version. Look up the details here.[8]

Verify your installation by typing the following command at the terminal:

```
$ crystal -v or $ crystal --version
```

This shows that you the installed version—for example: Crystal 0.26.1 [391785249] (2018-08-27) LLVM: 4.0.0 Default target: x86_64-unknown-linux-gnu

Now you're ready to go!

Compiling Code

After you've written your code in Ruby, you just run it. That's also true for Crystal. But under the hood, your code is first compiled to native code and then executed. During compilation, the Crystal compiler checks your code, and only when there are no errors, native code is generated and your code is run.

---

5.   https://github.com/faustinoaq/crystal-windows-installer
6.   https://github.com/crystal-lang/crystal/wiki/All-required-libraries
7.   https://github.com/crystal-lang/crystal
8.   https://crystal-lang.org/docs/installation/from_source_repository.html

For example, the following command:

```
$ crystal hello_world.cr
```

compiles and executes the code contained in the given source file. In fact, this is a shortcut, as compilation and execution are still two separate steps. If compilation fails, nothing will be run. This way of working is nice while developing small pieces, but the compiler has to do all that work again every time, so it's comparatively slow. To separate the compilation and execution steps, use the build option:

```
$ crystal build hello_world.cr
```

to generate a binary executable file, hello_world, which you can then execute with:

```
$ ./hello_world
```

To specify the executable filename as hello, use the –o flag:

```
$ crystal build -o hello hello_world.cr
```

For production-ready standalone executables or when performing benchmarks, you'll need to tell the compiler to create fully optimized code, which takes somewhat longer:

```
$ crystal build hello_world.cr --release --no-debug
```

(The –no-debug flag should be temporary and no longer be necessary in Crystal v1.0.)

If the platform you're using to do the builds doesn't match your production environment, then you're going to have to recompile it on the server. Another way to solve this is to deploy your app in a Docker container.

The crystal command can do a lot more. It contains a number of built-in tools, such as formatting code, generating a new project, and building its documentation. You can get an overview of what's possible by typing crystal on the command line as shown in the figure on page 197.

Explore the different compilation options with:

```
$ crystal build -h
```

Here are some things for you to try out.

Your Turn 1

➤ a. Compile hello_world.cr to an executable and compare the different file sizes in a normal build, a release build, and a build with debug-info.

```
ivo@ivo-SATELLITE-L50D-B:~/crystal-the-way-to/chapter 1$ crystal
Usage: crystal [command] [switches] [program file] [--] [arguments]

Command:
    init                    generate a new project
    build                   build an executable
    deps                    install project dependencies
    docs                    generate documentation
    env                     print Crystal environment information
    eval                    eval code from args or standard input
    play                    starts crystal playground server
    run (default)           build and run program
    spec                    build and run specs (in spec directory)
    tool                    run a tool
    help, --help, -h        show this help
    version, --version, -v  show version
```

➤ b. Compile test.cr with verbose error reporting and examine the output.

➤ c. Greet the world in Crystal by giving the code to the compiler on the command line itself. (Hint: Use crystal eval.)

➤ d. Find out how to view LLVM and assembler output by compiling hello_world.cr. (Don't worry: You won't need that for development.)

➤ e. Try out $ crystal env to see what info this gives.

➤ f. Experiment with icr,[9] the interactive console for Crystal. icr aims to be like irb for Ruby. It works differently under the hood because Crystal compiles instead of interpreting the code.

Clone the repository, switch to folder crystal-icr, and build it with the command: $ make.

Start it with: $ icr.

Type in a command at the icr > prompt and press ENTER to execute it. The UP ARROW gives access to previous commands, and CTRL-D exits. You'll probably be more charmed by the Crystal Playground. See *Working with Crystal Playground*, on page 200.

Using Editors and IDEs

You now know how to build and run a Crystal code file on the command line, but as a developer, you'll probably want some conveniences in your program editor, such as syntax-highlighting and other features. Plugins[10] exist for Emacs, Vim, Textmate, Notepad++, IntelliJ, Sublime Text, Atom, and Visual Studio Code. Also have a look here.[11]

---

9. https://github.com/crystal-community/icr
10. https://github.com/veelenga/awesome-crystal#editor-plugins
11. https://github.com/crystal-lang-tools

We'll highlight three cross-platform and open-source editors that offer IDE functionality for Crystal. The choice is yours—they all offer more or less the same developer support.

Working with Sublime Text

The well-known programmer's editor Sublime Text[12] has a nice plugin, Sublime-crystal,[13] that provides syntax highlighting and various forms of code completion. You can find it as *Crystal* in Sublime Text Package Control.

Install it with the menu Preferences / Package Control / Install Package. Then verify from the menu Tools / Build system that Crystal is checked.

After editing, you can build and execute a Crystal program with the keyboard combination CTRL+B. This saves your source code before you start to compile and run. But it also formats your source code by applying the crystal format tool, so your code is always in good shape!

In the code (hello_world_class.cr) in the screenshot that follows, I've defined a class HelloWorld with an initialize and a greet method. HelloWorld.new creates an object, hw, and this calls the greet method. This outputs the "Hello, world!" message. We'll go over syntax details in Chapter 2, *Crystal Foundations*, on page 19.

```
File  Edit  Selection  Find  View  Goto  Tools  Project  Preferences  Help

    hello_world_class.cr  x

 1  class HelloWorld
 2    def initialize(@name : String)
 3    end
 4
 5  def greet
 6      puts "Hello, #{@name}!"
 7    end
 8  end
 9
10  hw = HelloWorld.new("world")
11  hw.greet # => Hello, world!
12  |



Hello, world!
[Finished in 1.4s]
```

---

12. https://www.sublimetext.com/
13. https://github.com/crystal-lang/sublime-crystal

Working with Atom

Atom[14] is also a very popular editor, and there are no less than four plugins being developed for Crystal to enhance your developing experience. *ide-crystal* gives you an all-round package for working with Crystal, but some of the others might be good complements.

- ide-crystal[15] aims to provide all IDE functionality for Crystal, such as auto-completion, linting and formatting your code, and many more.
- language-crystal-actual[16] provides general Crystal language support, such as syntax highlighting and snippets.
- crystal-tools,[17] developed by Manas, enables the built-in Crystal compiler tools in Atom.
- crystal-block,[18] highlights matching crystal blocks for certain keywords.

The following is a screenshot with the same code as before:

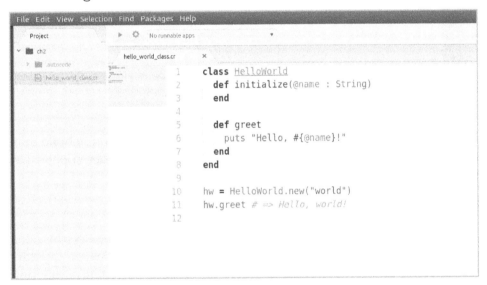

---

14. https://atom.io/
15. https://atom.io/packages/ide-crystal
16. https://atom.io/packages/language-crystal-actual
17. https://atom.io/packages/crystal-tools
18. https://atom.io/packages/crystal-block

Working with Visual Studio Code

Two Crystal plugins provide a nice IDE experience for Visual Studio Code:[19]

- vscode-crystal,[20] which adds code snippets and syntax highlighting as well as other options

- vscode-crystal-ide,[21] a Crystal IDE powered by Language Server Protocol, with syntax coloring and error checking, with many more features coming.

Here's a screenshot with the same code:

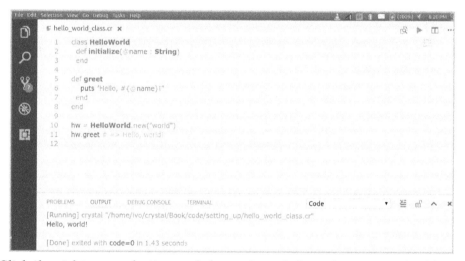

Click the right mouse button and choose Run code from the menu to build and run a code file. The vscode-native-debugger[22] provides debugger support for both GDB and LLDB.

Working with Crystal Playground

This tool is very useful if you want to quickly run and test some Crystal code, get instant feedback, understand its execution, try ideas, and teach Crystal. It's kind of a 21st-century version of a REPL-like irb, but it's built in JavaScript to run in the browser.

You must have Crystal installed on your machine for this. See the instructions earlier in this chapter to find out how.

Open up a terminal, and enter the command $ crystal play.

---

19. https://code.visualstudio.com/
20. https://github.com/g3ortega/vscode-crystal
21. https://github.com/kofno/crystal-ide
22. https://marketplace.visualstudio.com/items?itemName=webfreak.debug

You'll see this message: Listening on http://localhost:8080. Open up a browser with this URL, and you'll see the Playground with our familiar code:

The left pane is for code writing, editing, pasting, or dragging and dropping your code file. After you stop typing, the Playground will compile the code and execute it. You can speed things up by changing Time to wait in the Settings menu to 0.

Start with a specific code file by typing $ crystal play ./path/to/file.cr.

You'll be able to see every expression with its value in the right pane, so we'll often omit puts, print, or p statements in the book's code. For example, you'll see that the greet method, while running, will write the string "Hello, world!" to standard output. Helloworld.new creates an object (indicated by #<HelloWorld:memory_address>), and greet returns nil. Click on a line in the right pane to see a popup-window with values and their types.

If the program has output, you'll see it in the bottom pane. Click the >_ icon below the right pane. The editor stores your code in browser storage so that you can continue working on it in a later session.

When you want to execute code, press CTRL+ENTER or simply ENTER in the left pane, or push the large blue-green button in the bottom-right. When compiling, the center arrow changes into a stop button and a colored circle spins. Subsequently, any change in the editor pane also triggers the compilation.

When hovering over the blue button, two more icons appear: the upper to share the code as a gist, and a download button so you can save your code to a file.

Handling Errors

If the code contains an error, you'll see that message on a red background. Again, you can click on it to see more details:

```
class HelloWorld
  def initialize(@name : String)
  end

  def greet
    puts "Hello, #{name}!"
undefined local variable or method 'name'
  end
end

hw = HelloWorld.new("world")
hw.greet # => Hello, world!
instantiating 'HelloWorld#greet()'
```

Using a Workbook

Crystal provides you with the notebook functionality as in the Jupyter and Mathematica environments, where you can mix executable code and text documentation and presentation.

On the logo line, you'll see the menu items Playground, Workbook, and About, which contains a tutorial. Using a workbook is easy: create a folder called playground in the directory where you start up the $ crystal play server (probably your home folder). Inside the folder, create workbook files, which are .md Markdown files containing markdown and code. A code fragment is indicated like this:

```
```playground
# code fragment
```
```

Now you can access these files from the Workbook menu, which is handy for creating presentations and tutorials as shown in the figure on page 203.

See GitHub[23] for a recipe for building awesome presentations with the Playground.

How Does It Work?

When you execute the $crystal play command, a Crystal http server is started. In the Playground, your browser connects via a websocket to that http server,

---

23. https://github.com/crystal-lang/crystal-presents

and the code you type in is sent through it. The server processes the code and sends back the results (the –verbose flag shows the inner details).

Using Crystal Documentation

Finding answers when you're faced with coding questions or looking for possible solutions to problems is part of our job. Here[24] are some ways to ask questions directly to the community and the developers.

But before doing that, try to find your answer in the official documentation of the language and its standard library (API).

You'll find the docs of the core language in Gitbook form here.[25]

The search box in the upper-left corner is very useful:

---

24. https://crystal-lang.org/community/
25. https://crystal-lang.org/docs/

The standard library API[26] is also an indispensable resource when developing in Crystal.

From the main Crystal website, look up the term "hash" in the docs and in the standard library.

Wrapping Up

Congratulations! You've gained some experience with the Crystal compiler, and hopefully you've found a favorite editor for Crystal. Or perhaps you're a Crystal Playground convert. All of these will help you immerse yourself in Crystal code.

---

26. https://crystal-lang.org/api/

Porting Ruby Code to Crystal

Unfortunately, there isn't yet a migration tool from Ruby to Crystal, but converting Ruby code to Crystal is often quite straightforward. Consider the following:

- A lot of the dynamic power of Ruby does not exist in Crystal. This includes eval, send, instance_eval, auto_load, and define_method. Macros in Crystal can sometimes be used to achieve the same goal.

- Crystal also has less introspection—for example, methods doesn't exist on an object, though @type.methods works in macros.

- When overflow occurs in integer calculations, Ruby converts automatically from Fixnum to Bignum. Crystal 0.27, on the other hand, applies simple modular arithmetic. (Overflow is planned to appear in future versions of Crystal, however.)

The following table can help you to quickly convert Ruby code to Crystal:

From Ruby	To Crystal
NilClass	Nil
TrueClass, FalseClass	Bool
Fixnum	Int8, Int16, Int32, Int64, or same with U prefix
and	&&
or	||
Strings: " " or ' '	only " "
''	""
'"cute"'	"\"cute\"" or %{"cute"} or %("cute")
Heredoc: STR =<<DOC_NAME	STR = <<-DOC_NAME
for in	.each

From Ruby	To Crystal
trailing while or until	no equivalent, trailing if or unless
[]	[] of Type
{}	{} of KeyType => ValueType
$	$~.pre_match
$`	$~.post_match
&:	&.
attr_reader	getter
attr_writer	setter
attr_accessor	property
length, size, count	size
Enumerable#detect	Enumerable#find
Enumerable#collect	Enumerable#map
Enumerable#find_all	Enumerable#select (or grep if a regex pattern)
Enumerable#inject	Enumerable#reduce
fail	raise
File::exists?	File.exists?
File.readlines	File.read_lines
Hash.each_pair	Hash.each
include?	includes?
Kernel#proc	->
Kernel#lambda, Proc#new	->
lambda { |x|... }	->(x: Type) { ... }
Object#respond_to?	Object#responds_to?
require_relative "abc"	require "./abc"
class << self	def self.abc
private	private def
STDOUT.write	STDOUT.print
YAML.load	YAML.parse
"open-uri" open.readlines	"http/client" get(..).body.lines

Here[1] is a shard written by Faustino Aquilar to evaluate and assist in the porting of Ruby gems to Crystal.

Ruby Extensions in Crystal

Because the Ruby API is written in C, you can create Crystal bindings for the Ruby API and then write a Ruby gem in Crystal. Making this work reliably is not that easy, especially given that you will have to deal with garbage collection in both Crystal and Ruby. Paul Hoffer's crystalized_ruby[2] is a work in progress toward that end. This article[3] from Fabio Akita and this example[4] may help you get started.

---

1. https://github.com/faustinoaq/ruby2crystal
2. https://crystal.libhunt.com/project/crystalized_ruby
3. http://www.akitaonrails.com/2016/07/06/trying-to-match-c-based-fast-blank-with-crystal
4. https://gist.github.com/notozeki/7159a9d9ab9707a22129

Your Turn Answers

Some answers are provided here directly, but many are included in the exercises directory of the sample code[1]. If the answer looks like a file name ending in .cr, you'll want to check out the sample code.

Chapter 2: Crystal Foundations

Your Turn 1

```
12 + 12     # => 24
"12 + 12"   # => 12 + 12
"12" + "12" # => 1212
"I" * 5 # => "IIIII"
```

The following statements give compilation errors:

```
'12' + '12' # => unterminated char literal, use double quotes for strings
5 * "I"     # => no overload matches 'Int32#*' with type String
"12" + 12   # => no overload matches 'String#+' with type Int32
"2" * "5"   # => no overload matches 'String#*' with type String
```

Your Turn 2

delete.cr

Your Turn 3

empty.cr

1.　https://pragprog.com/titles/crystal/source_code

Your Turn 4

99_bottles_of_beer.cr

Your Turn 5

method.cr

Your Turn 6

a. union.cr

b. class.cr

Your Turn 7

For 500,000 fibers, I got:

$ crystal build fibers.cr --release

$ time ./fibers # => real 0m5.242s

Chapter 3: Typing Variables and Controlling the Flow

Your Turn 1

```
1_i8
16_i16
132
164_i64
264_u64
p int64 + int32 + uns64 # => 560_i64
p int8 + int64 # => -91_i8
```

Your Turn 2

a. splitting.cr

b. utf8.cr: The cat character 猫 has unicode codepoint 29483 and takes 3 bytes: 231, 140, and 171.

c. object_id.cr: Strings with the same value have the same object_id for performance. That id, of course, could differ from the value given here.

Integers have no object_id because they are created on the stack.

Your Turn 3

string_symbol.cr: They are not the same.

Your Turn 4

destructuring.cr

Your Turn 5

a. union_types.cr

b. hashes.cr

c. compile_runtime.cr

Your Turn 6

a. var1.cr: The value of var1 is 2; same output for a while instead of if.

b. if_elsif_else.cr: The output is 9 and has one digit.

c. exception_union.cr: The compile-time type of a is (Int32 | Nil); Nil is the type it had when an exception occurred. Use as to ease the compiler.

Chapter 4: Organizing Code in Methods and Procs

Your Turn 1

a. total.cr

b. splat_a_tuple.cr

Your Turn 2

syntax_sugar.cr

Your Turn 3

return_proc.cr

Your Turn 4

bubblesort.cr

Chapter 5: Using Classes and Structs

Your Turn 1

a. employee.cr

b. increment.cr

Your Turn 2

shape.cr

Your Turn 3

vec2d.cr

Your Turn 4

a. reopen.cr

b. reopen_method.cr

Chapter 6: Working with Modules

Your Turn 1

math_sin.cr

Your Turn 2

comparable2.cr

Chapter 7: Managing Projects

Your Turn 1

mineral (folder)

Your Turn 2

a. array_last_elem.cr

b. building_vs_concat.cr

Chapter 8: Advanced Features

Your Turn 1

def_method.cr

Your Turn 2

a. main_fiber3.cr

b. main_fiber4.cr

Chapter 9: Web Frameworks and the Shard Ecosystem

Your Turn 1

a. time_server.cr

b. index_server.cr

Appendix 1: Setting Up a Crystal Environment

Your Turn 1

a. hello_world.cr:

$ crystal build hello_world.cr # size: 1.1MB

$ crystal build hello_world.cr --release # size: 802KB (Use –release –no-debug if –release doesn't work for you.)

$ crystal build hello_world.cr --debug # size: 1.4MB

b. $ crystal build test.cr --error-trace

c. Put the code within single quotes: $ crystal eval 'puts "Greetings world!"' # => Greetings world!

d. $ crystal build hello_world.cr --emit llvm-ir/ (see file hello_world.ll)

$ crystal build hello_world.cr --emit asm (see file hello_world)

e. $ crystal env gives as output:

```
CRYSTAL_CACHE_DIR="/home/username/.cache/crystal"
CRYSTAL_PATH="lib:/opt/crystal/src"
CRYSTAL_VERSION="0.23.1"
```

f. A Crystal REPL: Clone the repository with $ git https://github.com/greyblake/crystal-icr.git.

Index

Thank you!

How did you enjoy this book? Please let us know. Take a moment and email us at support@pragprog.com with your feedback. Tell us your story and you could win free ebooks. Please use the subject line "Book Feedback."

Ready for your next great Pragmatic Bookshelf book? Come on over to https://pragprog.com and use the coupon code BUYANOTHER2019 to save 30% on your next ebook.

Void where prohibited, restricted, or otherwise unwelcome. Do not use ebooks near water. If rash persists, see a doctor. Doesn't apply to *The Pragmatic Programmer* ebook because it's older than the Pragmatic Bookshelf itself. Side effects may include increased knowledge and skill, increased marketability, and deep satisfaction. Increase dosage regularly.

And thank you for your continued support,

Andy Hunt, Publisher

The Joy of Programming

Put some fun back into your programming with these coding challenges. Generate custom mazes, and build your own ray tracer from scratch.

Mazes for Programmers

A book on mazes? Seriously?

Yes!

Not because you spend your day creating mazes, or because you particularly like solving mazes.

But because it's fun. Remember when programming used to be fun? This book takes you back to those days when you were starting to program, and you wanted to make your code do things, draw things, and solve puzzles. It's fun because it lets you explore and grow your code, and reminds you how it feels to just think.

Sometimes it feels like you live your life in a maze of twisty little passages, all alike. Now you can code your way out.

Jamis Buck
(286 pages) ISBN: 9781680500554. $38
https://pragprog.com/book/jbmaze

The Ray Tracer Challenge

Brace yourself for a fun challenge: build a photorealistic 3D renderer from scratch! It's easier than you think. In just a couple of weeks, build a ray tracer that renders beautiful scenes with shadows, reflections, brilliant refraction effects, and subjects composed of various graphics primitives: spheres, cubes, cylinders, triangles, and more. With each chapter, implement another piece of the puzzle and move the renderer that much further forward. Do all of this in whichever language and environment you prefer, and do it entirely test-first, so you know it's correct. Recharge yourself with this project's immense potential for personal exploration, experimentation, and discovery.

Jamis Buck
(270 pages) ISBN: 9781680502718. $45.95
https://pragprog.com/book/jbtracer

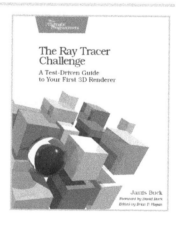

Level Up

From data structures to architecture and design, we have what you need for everyone on your team.

A Common-Sense Guide to Data Structures and Algorithms

If you last saw algorithms in a university course or at a job interview, you're missing out on what they can do for your code. Learn different sorting and searching techniques, and when to use each. Find out how to use recursion effectively. Discover structures for specialized applications, such as trees and graphs. Use Big O notation to decide which algorithms are best for your production environment. Beginners will learn how to use these techniques from the start, and experienced developers will rediscover approaches they may have forgotten.

Jay Wengrow
(220 pages) ISBN: 9781680502442. $45.95
https://pragprog.com/book/jwdsal

Design It!

Don't engineer by coincidence—design it like you mean it! Grounded by fundamentals and filled with practical design methods, this is the perfect introduction to software architecture for programmers who are ready to grow their design skills. Ask the right stakeholders the right questions, explore design options, share your design decisions, and facilitate collaborative workshops that are fast, effective, and fun. Become a better programmer, leader, and designer. Use your new skills to lead your team in implementing software with the right capabilities—and develop awesome software!

Michael Keeling
(358 pages) ISBN: 9781680502091. $41.95
https://pragprog.com/book/mkdsa

The Pragmatic Bookshelf

The Pragmatic Bookshelf features books written by developers for developers. The titles continue the well-known Pragmatic Programmer style and continue to garner awards and rave reviews. As development gets more and more difficult, the Pragmatic Programmers will be there with more titles and products to help you stay on top of your game.

Visit Us Online

This Book's Home Page
https://pragprog.com/book/crystal
Source code from this book, errata, and other resources. Come give us feedback, too!

Keep Up to Date
https://pragprog.com
Join our announcement mailing list (low volume) or follow us on twitter @pragprog for new titles, sales, coupons, hot tips, and more.

New and Noteworthy
https://pragprog.com/news
Check out the latest pragmatic developments, new titles and other offerings.

Save on the eBook

Save on the eBook versions of this title. Owning the paper version of this book entitles you to purchase the electronic versions at a terrific discount.

PDFs are great for carrying around on your laptop—they are hyperlinked, have color, and are fully searchable. Most titles are also available for the iPhone and iPod touch, Amazon Kindle, and other popular e-book readers.

Buy now at *https://pragprog.com/coupon*

Contact Us

Online Orders:	*https://pragprog.com/catalog*
Customer Service:	*support@pragprog.com*
International Rights:	*translations@pragprog.com*
Academic Use:	*academic@pragprog.com*
Write for Us:	*http://write-for-us.pragprog.com*
Or Call:	+1 800-699-7764

Milton Keynes UK
Ingram Content Group UK Ltd.
UKHW020145250324
439991UK00011B/1253